BIRDS of AFRICA

BIRDS of AFRICA

John Karmali

Foreword by Roger Tory Peterson

A STUDIO BOOK
The Viking Press · New York

To Joan

First published in 1980 by The Viking Press
625 Madison Avenue, New York, N.Y. 10022.

Published simultaneously in Canada by
Penguin Books Canada Limited

Library of Congress Cataloging in Publication Data
  Karmali, John, 1917–
    Birds of Africa

  (A Studio book)
  Bibliography: p.
  Includes index.
  1.   Birds––Africa––Pictorial works.
  2.   Photography of birds.
  I. Title.
QL692.AlK37 1980   598.296   80–5359
ISBN 0–670–16810–6

Designed and produced by
Adkinson Parrish Limited, London.

Managing Editor Clare Howell
Design Manager Christopher White

Editor Corinne Molesworth
Designer David Brown

Phototypeset in Great Britain by
Filmtype Services Limited, Scarborough

Colour illustrations originated in Italy by
Starf Photolitho SRL, Rome.

Printed in Hong Kong

Frontispiece   White-faced Tree Ducks
Dendrocygna viduata.
Page 7   A young Secretary Bird *Sagittarius
serpentarius* learning to fly from its nest in the
top of a thorn tree.
Page 19   A male Masai Ostrich *Struthio
camelus* at its nest.

Acknowledgements

Many people have helped me in various ways during the years it has taken to collect the material for this book. Without their assistance a work of this nature would not have been possible.

I must begin by paying tribute to the memory of the late Myles North, who inspired me to take up bird photography seriously, and encouraged me in my early days. Then always in the background there was Alec Forbes-Watson to advise, correct and guide me. Eric Hoskings's splendid books on bird photography provided the initial know-how and stimulus for this rather specialized technique.

No acknowledgements would be complete without the inclusion of Michael and Loretta Tremlett. Mike was a tower of strength in helping me to take advantage of numerous photographic situations, many of which he had himself discovered, and I shall always be grateful for their warm hospitality over many weekends. I think with gratitude of Jane and Tony Hopson, and John and Sandy Hopcraft who also provided hospitality and opportunities to photograph birds. I also hope that Dick and Angela Sparrow, Sol Rabb, and George Kinter, my companions on many safaris, think back with as much pleasure as I do to our various trips together.

My sincere thanks are due to them all; also to Peter Britton, Rena Fennessy, John Gerhart, Frants Hartmann, Richard Leakey, David Morris, Tony Pascoe, and Naresh and Mahesh Patel of Colorama for help and advice in various ways. I have left two important people until last. Firstly, Valerie Knowles who typed the manuscript twice, so efficiently and willingly, and my wife Joan for her continuous support, encouragement and inspiration.

Contents

Foreword

Some years ago, in preparation for my first African safari, I went into a chemist's shop in Nairobi. In addition to selling pharmaceutical supplies, it was also the sole distributor in East Africa for Leica cameras and was the place where sophisticated photographers bought much of their equipment and film. There I met the proprietor, John Karmali, who, it turned out, shared my passion for bird photography. He knew precisely what my needs were and was very helpful in suggesting where I might find certain birds. Since then, I have returned often to East Africa and have enjoyed a growing friendship with this gifted man.

A photographer who lives in a marvellous, interesting and photogenic country like Kenya has the advantage over someone who makes just a short visit. He can be on the spot when things are happening. This is undoubtedly why Allan Root's cine or motion picture films of Kenyan wildlife top anything taken by the best professional teams who come in on TV assignments. John Karmali has a similar advantage. His medium is still photography rather than cine and, although he will not pass up a good chance to document cheetahs, leopards, or lions, his real love, like mine, is birds.

Even a backyard in the suburbs of Nairobi can keep a bird photographer busy for days. Whereas in Britain, continental Europe, or North America, fifteen or twenty species might patronize a well-stocked suburban feeder, a person living in East Africa can attract at least twice that many, including attractive birds such as cordon-bleus, fire finches, and waxbills, as well as a variety of weavers and colourful starlings and even hornbills and barbets. Most of the national parks in East Africa – depending on the initiative of the manager – have installed feeding-trays for the pleasure of the guests. They may go out in the Landrover at daybreak to search for lions on a kill or to observe 'the big four' – the elephant, the rhino, the buffalo, and the hippo – but back at the lodge or tented camp, during the heat of the day and particularly during the lunch hour, they can watch the pageantry of the birds. At Kilaguni, golden-breasted starlings, red-billed hornbills, and buffalo weavers gather on the long veranda to be fed by the guests. At Samburu even fan-tailed ravens will come within arm's length, as well as a host of other exciting birds.

The colourful rollers and bee-eaters are not as trusting, but a long lens, preferably a 400mm, will pull them in. Not every time, of course. I found that if I was persistent I might eventually find an amenable individual. I would try to approach three or four rollers without getting close enough, but the fifth or sixth one, as often as not, would be tamer and more cooperative. There is no part of the world where the bird enthusiast or the bird photographer can enjoy a happier or more successful holiday than in East Africa.

Australia is marvellous too, with its parrots, often rather tame, and its honey-eaters and kookaburras; but in East Africa one is offered an even greater galaxy of photographic subjects, ranging from tiny finches to huge vultures and massive congregations of pelicans and other water birds. The lakes of the Rift Valley literally swarm with birds. The saline lakes, such as Nakuru and Elmenteita with their vast flocks of flamingos have an avifauna quite unlike that of nearby freshwater lakes such as Naivasha.

John Karmali, who met his wife, Joan, while studying pharmacy at London University, is one of Nairobi's most public-spirited citizens. He has been witness to the social struggles and progress of his beloved Kenya from the days before Uhuru to the present time and he himself has played no small part in social reform, community affairs, and education.

His interest in wildlife, especially birds, has led to active participation in the East African Natural History Society, the Nakuru Wildlife Trust, the World Wildlife Fund, the Kenya National Museum, and the National Parks system for which he once served as a trustee. He has enjoyed a lifetime of experience with the birds of East Africa and has added much to our knowledge of them. So the chemist has become the conservationist. In addition to his many natural history involvements he has also served as an alderman of the City Council of Nairobi and has long been active in the Rotary Club of which he is now chairman.

This book reveals still another facet of this multi-talented man. Like many another nature-oriented person he finds much pleasure and relaxation in photography. By blending his technical expertise and knowledge of birds with a good eye for aesthetics, he has distinguished himself as one of East Africa's foremost wildlife photographers. His salon prints have earned him a fellowship in the Royal Photographic Society of Great Britain.

In earlier years the object of going on safari in East Africa was to shoot. Today, because of conservationists like John Karmali, shooting is being replaced by the more civilized sport of photographing – or just looking. Because the herds of big game are dwindling outside the parks and reserves, tourists find increasing pleasure in the spectacular bird life. Well over 1000 species are found in the relatively small country of Kenya. This book is a showcase of John Karmali's work and should inspire the avid bird enthusiast from Europe or North America to board the next plane bound for this exciting continent.

Roger Tory Peterson

Preface

Strangely enough, the most frequent questions put to me during my exhibition of bird photographs in February 1974 were not about how I took them, but *why* I took them. 'Why photograph birds? What made you concentrate on birds instead of mammals?' Having to find answers to these questions made me search for the basic reasons why today I devote most of my time to this aspect of photography. This meant going right back to those years when I first started taking photography seriously.

From childhood I have always been keen on art, but education in Kenya in the twenties and thirties had its limitations, and untrained teachers did little to develop any latent talent I may have had. Although I tried to study art privately when I first went to England in the mid-thirties, I soon became completely involved in working for my future profession as a pharmacist and there was no time left for art. So I could well be described as a frustrated artist. In 1939 I bought my first camera, purely as a recording instrument. It was not until 1943, when I got married, that I bought my first 'serious' camera: a Leica. My wife gave me, then as now, her complete and enthusiastic support for my efforts at photography.

I soon realized the artistic possibilities of this beautiful precision camera and because it satisfied my desire to create, I became an enthusiastic photographer. Turning my attention to serious pictorial photography, I decided that a keen photographer would never consider having films processed commercially, so I started doing my own developing and printing. It was still wartime, materials were in short supply, but slowly and steadily my processing technique improved. My training as a pharmacist was of great value and my later training in optics helped me to understand the importance of light and its use in the formation of the photographic image. In England I concentrated mainly on landscape photography. The atmospheric effects produced in town and country by the changing seasons; by mist and soft shadows; by the long shadows in the mornings and evenings attracted and enchanted me. I spent a great deal of time trying to capture these fleeting effects on film, with rare but occasionally rewarding success.

Returning to Kenya in 1946, having completed my studies in England, I continued with my efforts at pictorial photography, but gradually dissatisfaction set in. Kenya sits astride the equator, mists are rare, the sun climbs rapidly overhead to throw hard shadows and the seasons show little atmospheric variation. I soon discovered, to my regret, that it was not possible to do the type of landscape photography in Kenya which gave me such satisfaction in England. But Kenya had something else to offer – game photography – and so I turned to this. At about this time, my wife and I were fortunate in getting to know Dr Louis B. Leakey, a friend we shall always remember with great affection. He not only introduced me to the East African Natural History Society but persuaded me to join its executive committee, whose chairman at the time was Dr E. Barton Worthington. This was my introduction to the natural history of this country, creating an interest which has continued to grow over the years and has formed an important adjunct to my wildlife photography. One can never get tired of photographing animals. It may well happen that, after the 500th exposure, the more common mammals do not seem so photogenic, but the element of surprise and luck is always present. The first time one observes a leopard with its kill on a tree, a cheetah with its young under a bush or a giraffe with a back-cloth of majestic Kiliminjaro, are highlights of a game photographer's life.

Sitting quietly out in the bush I occasionally saw and photographed the larger birds such as the Crowned Cranes, Ostriches, Secretary Birds and sometimes smaller birds as well, but not very seriously or with any degree of success. Then fate took a hand. Myles E. W. North was anxious to make photographic records of the courting, nesting and other behaviour of a Black Heron colony in Nairobi, and asked for my help. Thanks to this, I developed a deep curiosity about birds and began to photograph them. It was not until the late forties that I began to pay particular attention to the making of colour transparencies. I recall processing early Anscochrome films in my home darkroom at this time, with some rather startling and unexpected results.

To a frustrated artist, colour photography might seem to be the obvious answer, but it did not fully satisfy the creative urge. Home-processing was too uncertain and commercial-processing gave one no sense of involvement in the final result. On the other hand, making one's own enlargements from black-and-white negatives was highly satisfying, and to this day I continue to do some black-and-white photography for this reason.

I soon found that I knew very little of the specialized techniques of bird photography. Oliver Pike's books on the subject were of interest, but it was from Eric Hosking, the world-famous bird photographer, that I learned most. His book *Bird Photography as a Hobby*, written with Cyril Newberry in 1961, was invaluable and gave me a great deal of very useful information on the technique of building hides or blinds, and using other methods for getting close to birds. Eric has become a good friend of mine in recent years.

Trying to apply my newly-acquired knowledge, I soon discovered that bird photography in East Africa was rather different from that in Europe. Basic techniques were similar, but these had to be modified to meet the special conditions in Kenya. Next it became evident that to be really successful, one needed a great deal of knowledge about the birds themselves and their behaviour patterns at different times. Now an active member of the East African Natural History Society, I improved my knowledge of ornithology with sympathetic help from its members and particularly from Alec Forbes-Watson.

I find I am happiest when completely engrossed in trying to photograph a bird in its natural environment. But photographing to record, to be able to capture on film yet another species, is not enough. Once the technical side of photography has become almost automatic, after many years of practical experience, it is the creative, aesthetic aspect which is important. And so I come to the essence of my motivation and what might be regarded as my particular philosophy of bird photography. I do not intend to get involved in the never-ending controversy as to whether photography is art and whether the results are creative. However, if art can be described as 'the production or expression of what is beautiful, appealing or of more than ordinary significance', I see no objection to the camera and film being one more medium for producing a work of art.

I shall now try to outline what to me are the significant aspects of my style and to explain the techniques I have evolved. Because the camera is mechanical, it can and does interfere with one's creative ability, unless the techniques of using it are mastered. A good book on photography can give one all the information necessary for producing a technically good photograph. Continuous practice is important and it is essential that, in the early stages, notes are kept on exposures and lenses used etc., and the final results examined carefully to find out what went wrong or even right! It takes time, then suddenly one discovers that the mechanics have become almost automatic, and the mind is free to concentrate on creating the picture.

And from there, the photographer, like any other artist, is on his own. He can follow his instincts, or if more seriously inclined, can examine the work of other photographers; look at works of art and read about them; study colour composition and colour balance, to widen his knowledge. His own individual style will gradually emerge. At the time of releasing the shutter he alone, like a painter, can visualize the end-result. Technique has to be perfect. The smallness of the 35mm transparency, which has to be enlarged considerably for projection or reproduction, leaves no room for errors. The focussing must be exact, there should be no camera shake, and the exposure must be correct for the desired end-result. Even so, a technically correct exposure may not necessarily have the impact that the photographer has in mind when he presses the button. In order to achieve a three-dimensional effect, it is very important to separate the subject from the background; this will, I hope, be obvious in a number of examples in this book. This differential focussing is achieved by using as wide an aperture as possible; the Three-banded Plover, plate 36, is a good illustration of this. With a smaller aperture and consequent greater depth of field, the reeds in the background would have been sharper and thus in conflict with the bird.

I go to a great deal of trouble to ensure that backgrounds harmonize with their subjects. This often necessitates trying different camera positions until the right effect is obtained. Because of this need to match the setting to the subject I rarely use a flash, which brightly illuminates the subject and not the background, thus giving the impression that the exposure was made at night. The final result is not true to nature and so unsatisfactory. Sometimes the use of a flash is unavoidable, especially with birds at nests located in dark surroundings, but the result very rarely satisfies my criteria of creative photography. A bird does not have to be particularly colourful to make an attractive composition. A number of my favourite pictures, some of which are illustrated here, are almost monochromatic.

I compose my picture in the viewfinder at the time of making the exposure. Unlike black-and-white photography, where the negative is but an intermediate step, colour slides are themselves the end-product and do not allow for any degree of manipulation. Also the 35mm format is already so small that 'cropping' is impractical. The answer is to fill the frame with the exact amount of subject matter visualized in the end-result. A photographer, unlike a painter, cannot leave out a tree, or move a hill to modify the landscape. All he can do is alter his viewpoint. The final picture may not follow the recognized rules of composition, but rules are made to be broken and thus help to create an individual style. It has become a standing joke among my friends that I consider it absolutely vital to get the highlight in the eye of the bird. It is amazing how this adds 'life' to the photograph.

My favourite lens, which has a focal length of 280mm, is generally considered to be rather small for photographing birds, especially passerines, and even bigger birds when not at their nests. However, rather than use a longer lens, I prefer to try to get closer to the subject by using hides or blinds, or other means. The 280mm lens is much easier to manipulate and offers its own challenge in that one has to get that much nearer to fill the frame. I do use longer lenses occasionally, where there is no alternative, but I do so with reluctance. Producing a pleasing and satisfying photograph is a matter of overcoming a number of challenges. The fact that my transparency is commercially produced is no longer of any particular significance. The creative urge has already been satisfied while considering and overcoming the many problems which precede the making of a successful exposure.

Introduction

I was awakened during the night by the Hadada Ibis complaining raucously at being disturbed by someone near their roost at the bottom of our garden. As I lay in bed listening to the various sounds of the night, I heard the plaintive, drawn-out notes of the Abyssinian Nightjar, and the territorial hoot of the Barn Owl, which had been living in our chimney for some months, before the weather turned cold and fires had to be lit.

As dawn came, I was aware of the Olive Thrush, which always seems to be the first bird to sing in our garden; next the Robin Chat took up its refrain. I could picture it sitting upright on a branch, puffing out its orange breast as it ran through its musical repertoire. In the valley the Helmeted Guineafowl were foraging for food and providing a chorus of loud, repeated cackles. Soon a White-browed Coucal or water-bottle bird joined in with its characteristic bubbling song. Next came the cry of the Red-throated Wryneck, the distant call of the Black Cuckoo and the sparrow-like chirping of a pair of Reichenow's Weavers. It dawned on me at that moment that this widely disparate variety of birds was being heard only six miles from the centre of Nairobi, the capital of Kenya!

This abundance of birds is not confined to Kenya or even East Africa: the whole continent is rich in its avifauna. For the purpose of this book, Africa is defined as that area of the continent which lies south of the Sahara. This desert area forms a natural barrier separating the two major faunal regions of Euro-Asia and Africa, the former known as the Palaearctic Region and the latter as the Ethiopian Region (not to be confused with the single territory of Ethiopia in north-eastern Africa).

There are over 9000 species of birds in the world, divided into 173 families of which the Ethiopian Region has eighty-seven, made up of about 1750 species, including migrants. Eleven families of the region are endemic, meaning that they are confined specifically to this area. East Africa (made up of Kenya, Uganda and Tanzania) has 1293 species, including 159 Palaearctic migrants; eighty-five families and ten endemic families. Kenya itself has the richest avifauna of any country on the African continent.

It is possible for a bird-watcher confined to a twenty-five-mile radius of Nairobi to see over 100 species in a single day: over 50 per cent of the country's birds have been recorded in this area. Kenya's bird species are exceeded in the world only by those of Colombia, Venezuela and Peru, but the majority of the South American species, unlike those of Kenya, are forest birds and therefore not so readily seen. A variety of factors are responsible for the extensive avifauna in Africa and especially East Africa, and it may be of interest to look at some of them.

Geographical Distribution

The distribution of bird species throughout the world is determined by a number of factors, which include climate and its effect on vegetation, and the physical structure of the land-mass and its terrain. The study of these factors is called zoogeography, and the major zoogeographic regions of the world are shown in the map Figure 1 on page 12.

When studying distribution, one might assume that different species would be confined to different land-masses. A large mass of water can and does form a barrier, but in fact the distribution of species is not always limited by this factor. In Africa, it is the Sahara, rather

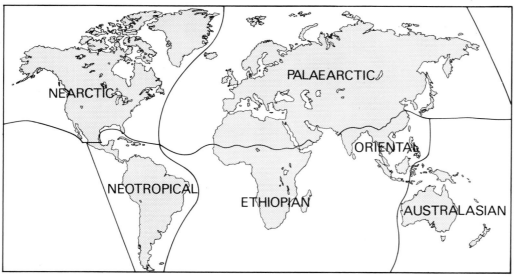

Figure 1 Zoogeographic Regions of the World.

than the Mediterranean, which forms the demarcation in the dispersal of avifauna between the European and African continents.

The concept of zoogeographic regions arose from the need to relate these different distributions to areas not necessarily defined by existing continents. In 1857, P. L. Sclater divided the world population of birds into six different regions: the Palaearctic, comprising Europe, North Africa and northern Asia; the Nearctic, comprising North America; the Neotropical, including Central and South America; the Oriental, made up of tropical Asia and Western Indonesia; the Australasian, comprising Australia, New Zealand and adjacent islands, and the Ethiopian consisting of Africa south of the Sahara. The boundaries between regions are not always clearly defined, as overlapping occurs in the transitional zones.

Palaearctic Region

A large number of Palaearctic species (almost a third of them) migrate to spend their winter non-breeding season in the Ethiopian Region. Millions of years ago the low-lying and marshy areas which formed much of what is now Europe and Asia had a warm, temperate climate. When the ice-age came, it destroyed forests and grasslands, forcing the animals and birds to move south. When in time the ice receded, grassy plains and woodlands gradually replaced the tundra which had been left after glaciation. Although numerous birds returned to occupy their former territories, the species count for this region is surprisingly low, being about half that of Africa, because of climatic changes brought about by glaciation.

Today this region is made up of Europe, Asia north of the Himalayas, and Africa north of the Sahara (see Figure 1 page 12). Its boundaries are the Arctic, the Atlantic and the Pacific Oceans, and the Sahara. Through the long weeks of summer, the vast treeless plains of the arctic regions of Europe and Asia teem with insect life and the wetlands are lush with vegetation. They sustain a large number of birds, which invade the area every year, but come the inhospitable weather, and they are away to the south. As many as 3750 million of them may head for the Ethiopian Region.

The Sahara This is the largest desert in the world covering about 3,500,000 square miles of North Africa, from the Mediterranean south to Sudan and from the Atlantic east to the Red Sea. It is a land of great severity, temperatures ranging from freezing at night to searing heat during the day, with an average yearly rainfall of less than four inches. Vegetation is sparse, mainly occurring at isolated oases. Of the twenty-five typical desert species which have adapted to these inhospitable conditions, over a third are sandgrouse and larks.

The Palaearctic migrants which made the Mediterranean crossing are faced with the formidable 1000-mile-wide barrier of the Sahara. Conditions are so arid that they cannot obtain any food or drink except in the small, isolated oases. A wide variety of species make what is possibly the most arduous journey made by migrants anywhere in the world, though at a price. Swallows, for example, suffer losses of nearly three out of five adults.

Ethiopian Region

The Ethiopian Region covers an area of approximately 8,000,000 square miles. Most of it lies between the tropics of Cancer and Capricorn and is characterized by high temperatures throughout the year and pronounced wet and dry seasons.

The northern boundary is not so readily defined as the desert gradually extends into it, but most of it lies between 18° to 20° N lat. About 500,000 square miles lie south of the tropics extending to 35° S lat.

The highly diversified topography, varying from sea level to mountains nearly 20,000 feet high, and the variation in climate with the consequent variation in vegetation, determine the distribution of species over this region.

Physical Characteristics

The relief map Figure 2 on page 14 shows the contrasting range of altitudes of the Ethiopian Region. A broken range of highlands runs down the eastern side of the African continent from the Red Sea to Cape Province. Most of the surface of Africa, which lies between the tropics, consists of savanna or wooded steppe. There are a large number of isolated mountains forming pockets of ecological interest, with particular vegetation and avifauna.

These highlands start from the broad spine of Ethiopia and spread through Uganda, Kenya and Tanzania. Important high mountains in this area are the Ruwenzori on the north-west border of Uganda; Elgon on the borders of Kenya and Uganda; Mount Kenya; and Meru and Kilimanjaro (19,340 feet high) in northern Tanzania. In the southern third of Africa, most of the land is over 3000 feet; in the east an almost continuous chain of mountains runs from Malawi to Cape Province, and includes the 600-mile-long Drakensberg chain. In the west are the separate highlands of the Benguela province in Angola, and those of South-west Africa.

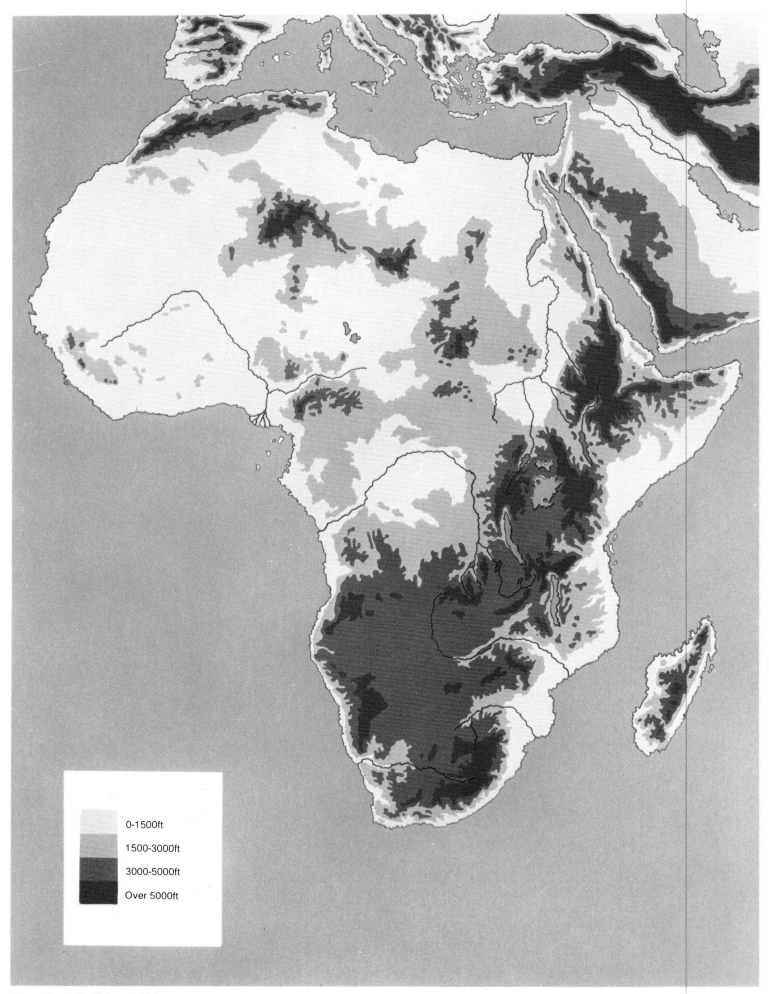

0-1500ft

1500-3000ft

3000-5000ft

Over 5000ft

Figure 2 Relief Map of Africa.

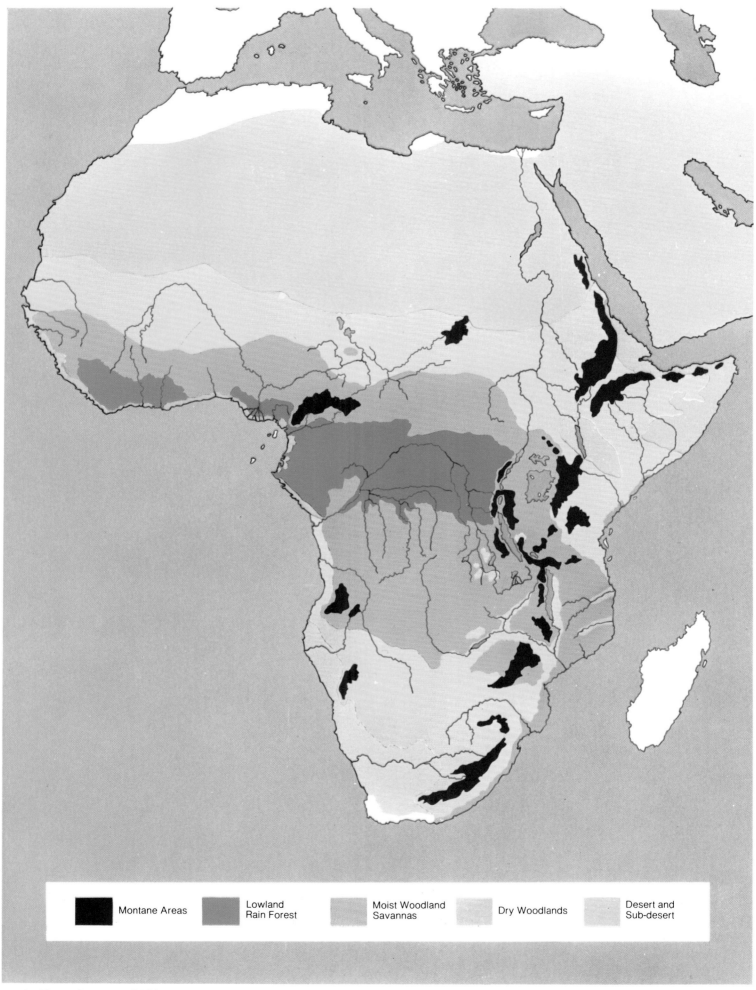

Figure 3 Vegetation Map of Africa.

West and Central Africa north of the equator differ from the areas previously described in that most of the land is below 1500 feet, only some of it rising up to 3000 feet. Far away in the west a small isolated range of mountains appears in the Cameroons, of which Mount Mouti in the Bamenda highlands reaches 8790 feet, and even more dramatically, the volcano Mount Cameroon on the coast of Cameroon towers to the height of 13,370 feet. There is a marked similarity between the avifauna of the mountain areas of Angola and the Cameroons and that of the Great Rift Valley, widely separated as they are. Long ago, when the rims of the Congo Basin were much higher than they are today, they probably formed part of a bridge linking the mountains of the east and west.

Most of the million square miles of the low-lying Sudan is a semi-desert, as are the coastal areas of Somalia, parts of eastern Ethiopia and north-eastern Kenya. A true desert called the Namib lies in the south-west coastal belt of southern Africa extending for about 900 miles. The coastal parts of Mozambique, and large areas of South-west Africa and Botswana including the waterless Kalahari, are also semi-desert. The major part of the rest of the Region is divided between grasslands, savanna woodlands and forest. Primaeval forest occurs only in isolated patches in the highlands, mountain valleys, and along river banks.

The major rivers of the Ethiopian Region such as the Niger, the Congo, the two Niles and the Zambezi influence the continent's birdlife indirectly. Most of the rivers are seasonal, rising during the rains and inundating vast areas with flood waters, forming swamps which are ideal habitats for ducks, waders and other aquatic birds. Typical examples are the shallow swamps of the Kafue River in Zambia and the upper Niger. During the dry season the rivers fall exposing sandbanks, and species such as bee-eaters and pratincoles take advantage of these safe nesting sites.

Of the three large lakes that show up so distinctly on the map, neither Lakes Malawi nor Tanganyika, with their great depth and steep sides, are of any major value to birds but Lake Victoria, the second largest freshwater lake in the world, is a different matter. This shallow lake, the source of the White Nile, attracts on average over fifty inches of annual rainfall. This encourages a rich vegetation on its periphery which supports a large variety of birdlife. The small alkaline lakes in the Great Rift Valley, particularly those in eastern Africa, provide a specialized habitat for a few species, notably the flamingo.

Rainfall
Rainfall is mentioned here because of its effect on vegetation and thus on the distribution of birds. Most of the region receives its annual rainfall in a single rainy season; where lowland rainforests exist in a narrow belt around the equator (see the vegetation map Figure 3 on page 15), it rains throughout the year, with an average of 60 to 80 inches. One of the wettest areas is the seaward side of Mount Cameroon where the annual rainfall can reach at least 160 inches. Desert and sub-desert areas average below 10 inches and the remainder of the region gets between 10 and 60 inches. The general pattern of rainfall is modified by mountains, which impose their own local pattern, and also by the adjacent coastal weather.

Vegetation Birds which live in evergreen forests are not usually found in non-forest areas, and few of the species found at high altitudes frequent low-lying plains. The distinction between typically montane and typically lowland birds is an important characteristic of Africa. Figure 3 on page 15 shows the location of the four main types of vegetation which influence distribution.

Lowland Rainforests These occur in a narrow band on the equator where there is no marked dry season. These forests are most dense on the west coast where the rains are heaviest; moving eastwards they get more and more sparse until along the eastern side of the region, even on the equator, the conditions at these low altitudes prove too dry for them to occur. This type of forest consists of trees between 100 and 150 feet in height, forming an overhead canopy, with few, if any, low side branches; little vegetation grows on the heavily shaded ground beneath. At this level and somewhat higher can be found some species of game birds, such as guineafowls and francolins, and a variety of thrush-like birds including babblers. The richer higher levels may contain cuckoos, turacos, trogons, hornbills, barbets, starlings, flycatchers and certain weavers. If the canopy is broken by the fall of a tree, a secondary growth of specially adapted plants appears and this is utilized by other species of birds. Therefore man-made clearings, to a limited extent, enrich the avifauna of such forests. Typical forests are those of the Congo Basin and coastal areas of West Africa.

Savannas Large parts of Africa have well-marked, alternating wet and dry seasons, though the wet may last as long as nine months. Characteristic vegetation in these areas consists of deciduous trees and perennial grasses. Where the rainfall is heaviest at the edge of lowland forests, these trees form great areas of dry woodlands in the southern tropics called 'miombo'; elsewhere the trees are scattered through the grasslands forming typical savanna country. These trees have adapted to survive the fierce fires which occur in the dry seasons.

Some authorities further divide the savannas into 'woodland savannas', which exist in the

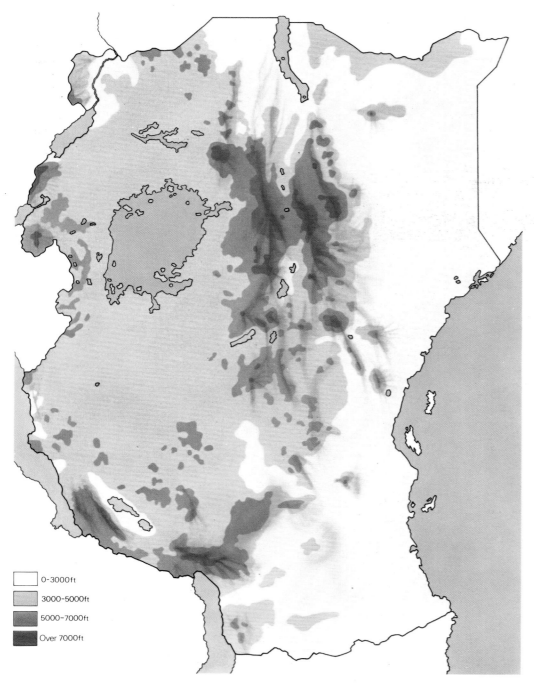

Figure 4 Relief Map of East Africa.

0-3000ft
3000-5000ft
5000-7000ft
Over 7000ft

moister areas north and south of the equator and immediately adjacent to the rainforests, and 'dry woodlands'. The latter form parallel belts further north and south between the woodland savannas and semi-deserts, and along part of the east side of the Region.

Characteristic birds of this habitat are a number of species of grass-warblers and weavers. Water channels meander through the savannas; on their banks fruit trees attract birds.

Montane areas A characteristic of much of the Ethiopian Region is the marked change that takes place, both in the animal and plant population, above 5000 feet; this altitude marks the beginning of the montane areas. Some of these areas are not forested; those which are contain evergreen species which do not grow as tall or dense as those in lowland forests. The avifauna of these areas is peculiar to them and shows no close relationship to the birds of the surrounding lowlands. Although these birds are so isolated, they are often found in similar montane areas hundreds of miles away.

Semi-dry zones The rainfall in these scrubby areas is so scarce that non-woody vegetation appears only after the rains. Coursers, bustards and larks are common here.

East Africa

Having seen how topography and the influence of climate on vegetation affects the distribution of avifauna, it is no wonder that the birdlife of East Africa is so rich. The physical geography of this area is complicated and highly diversified, extending from sea level to high mountains. The map Figure 4 on page 18 shows the series of plateaux at altitudes which range from 1300 to 10,000 feet; the contrasting higher regions of Central

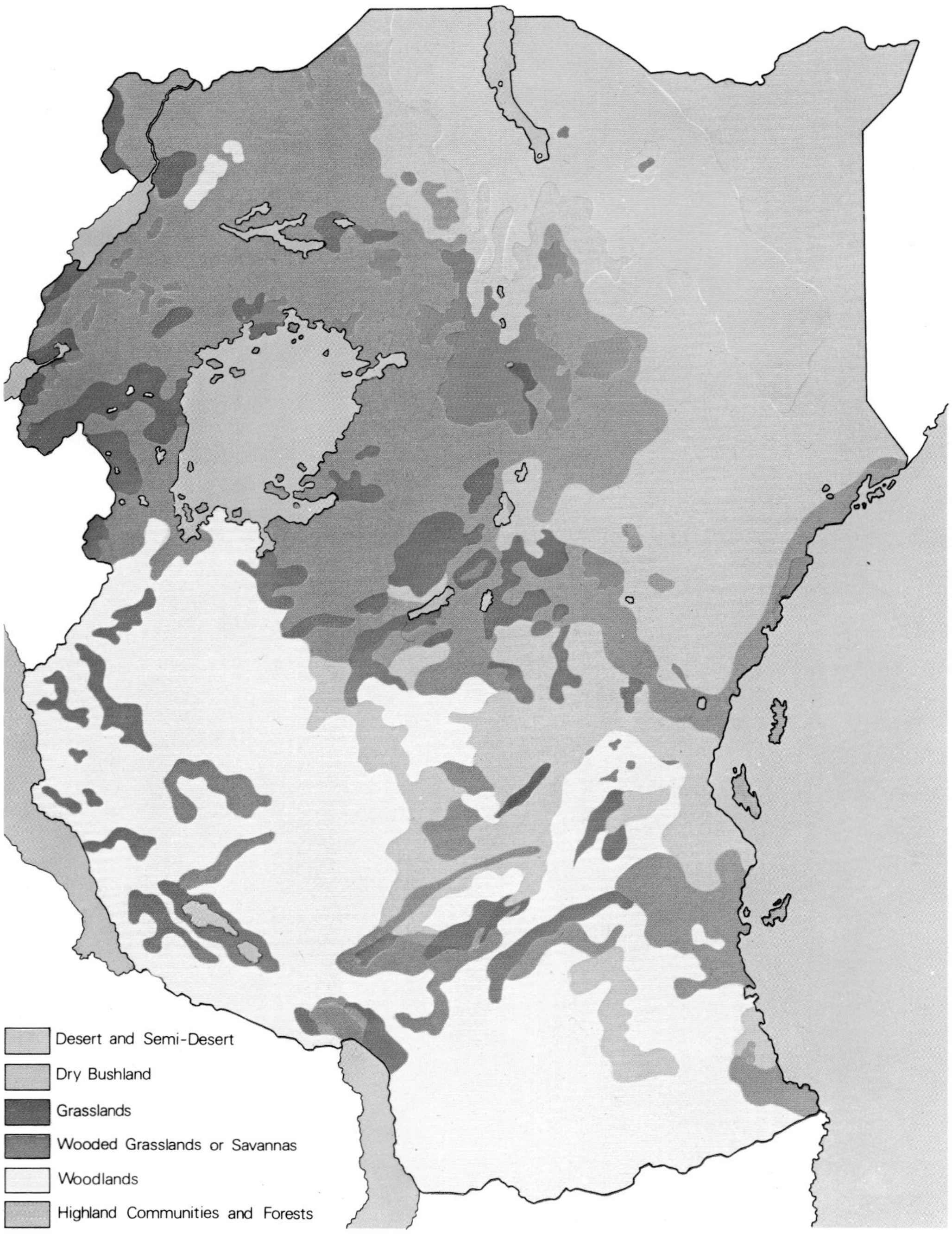

Figure 5 Vegetation Map of East Africa.

Desert and Semi-Desert
Dry Bushland
Grasslands
Wooded Grasslands or Savannas
Woodlands
Highland Communities and Forests

Kenya, south-western Uganda, the Northern and Southern Highlands of Tanzania and the Ruwenzori Mountains with their highest point, the Kibo peak of Kilimanjaro (19,340 feet).

Climate Because of the great range of altitudes, the wide distribution of lakes, high and desert land barriers, air movements and ocean currents, East Africa shows marked climatic differences. Three distinct rainfall seasons occur in different parts of the region.

Vegetation East Africa provides an almost complete range of habitats, from desert to savanna and from highland grasslands to montane areas. The map Figure 5 on page 19 shows the distribution of the various types of vegetation. Although the main lowland rainforests exist on the wetter, western side of the continent, there are vestigial patches of Congo-type forest on the eastern side, in coastal and near-coastal pockets. The scarcity of these patches of forest and the consequent rarity of their avifauna, similar to the birds in the western evergreen areas, make it essential that they should be preserved.

The non-forest zones that lie between the mountains and the evergreen forest of the lowlands, provide a variety of habitats and support the largest number of bird species. These zones include various types of savanna from thickish wooded savanna in the wetter areas, to the drier, open, grassy country. Level low-lying plains that flood during the rainy season encourage a heavy growth of vegetation, and the breeding of numbers of weavers. Much of East Africa is made up of typical montane regions, the land being over 5000 feet.

From harsh tracts of desert, to rolling grasslands and towering mountains, this immense and diverse continent thus encompasses many types of habitat. A meeting-place for vast numbers of native and migrant birds, the region truly supports 'an abundance of birds'.

1 Ostriches

Almost all birds fly, but amongst the few that do not is an important group of birds known as ratites. They have a number of characteristics which are more primitive in comparison with most other living birds. This led some people to believe that, during their evolution, the ratites had branched off from the main stem of all other birds before the latter had evolved the power of flight. However, many of the structural features of the ratites, such as the fact that they all have a wing skeleton which is not fundamentally different from that of flying birds, indicate that they are descendants from the latter.

Although these running, flightless birds show common features associated with the loss of flight, such as the fusion together of the bones of the shoulder girdle and the absence of the keel of the sternum, they are not closely related. The Kiwi of New Zealand, the Rhea of South America, the Emu and Cassowary of Australia and the Ostrich of Africa belong to the four different orders of living ratites.

The ostrich *Struthio camelus* is the only living representative of the family Struthionidae and has the distinction of being a member of one of only two orders confined exclusively to Africa (the other is the mousebird). It is the largest among living birds, the adult male standing nearly 8 feet high and weighing over 300 pounds. The body plumage is black, and the wings and tail are white. The head, neck and legs are bare of feathers, and the colour of the naked long neck and strong thighs varies from pink to bluish grey depending upon the race. The female is somewhat smaller, with a greyish-brown body, wings and tail. An attractive feature is the presence of very prominent thick black eyelashes, surrounding an eyeball 2 inches across.

Evolved for running, its powerful legs end, unlike those of other ratites, in only two toes: a large strongly clawed third toe and a weaker clawless fourth or outside toe. The first and second toes are missing. This adaptation to efficient running is illustrated by the fact that an ostrich can maintain a steady speed of about thirty miles per hour for almost half an hour and can reach bursts of over forty miles per hour to outstrip most pursuers. The wings are used mainly for display, quite often very energetic and spectacular. It is usually silent, but during the breeding season the male produces a deep booming call, presumably to indicate its territory.

Of the five sub-species (races) inhabiting various parts of Africa, the three most numerous are the better known Masai Ostrich which lives on the grassy plains of southern Kenya and Tanzania and has pink thighs and neck, the Somali race which ranges from north of the Tana River in eastern Kenya to Somalia and southern Ethiopia, and the

Right, Plate 2 A female Masai Ostrich *Struthio camelus*.
Below This female Masai Ostrich is in the process of swallowing food, indicated by the thickening of the upper part of its neck.
Below left Conspicuous because of their magnificent plumage, ostriches rely on being able to outrun their predators.

Overleaf, top left This male Masai Ostrich cannot possibly cover the widespread clutch, so the unbrooded eggs will fail to hatch.
Top right A male stalks the ground foraging for food, its upraised foot clearly showing the two toes that enable it to run so fast.
Bottom, Plate 3 Male Masai Ostrich *Struthio camelus*.

Southern Ostrich which is found in south-western Africa. The Somali and Southern Ostriches two sub-species have greyish-blue neck and thighs.

Ostriches live in a wide variety of habitats from semi-desert to wooded savanna. In East Africa they are often found in association with plains game such as zebra, wildebeest, gazelle and sometimes giraffe. They are usually seen in small parties of up to ten, but when accompanied by females and young birds, the numbers may reach as many as fifty. They are subject to predation by carnivores, the chicks being particularly vulnerable. The adult with its keen eyesight and turn of speed can generally make a getaway.

Sometimes described as omnivorous, their diet consists mainly of vegetable matter, such as succulents, shrubs, berries and seeds, although a certain amount of animal matter such as lizards etc. is also swallowed accompanied by a quantity of grit to aid digestion by helping to grind up the food. There is no truth in the belief that ostriches can manage for long periods without water and are therefore able to live in desert country. Water is essential and in semi-desert areas, moisture is obtained from green vegetation.

The male is polygamous and may have as many as five different hens though three is a more usual number. The eggs are laid by all of them in one nest, usually a hollow in the ground, at the rate of one every other day up to eight eggs. The nest may therefore contain between twenty and forty eggs, but as many as fifty have been recorded. Eggs are creamy white with a very thick shell and are smooth in some sub-species, and rough and pitted in others. They are 6 inches by 5 inches in size; their weight is equal to approximately twenty-five hens' eggs and they are said to be good to eat, taking forty minutes to hard boil.

Incubation which takes about forty days is carried out mainly by the cock, but the dominant hen takes over for some of the daylight hours. A large proportion of the clutch fails to hatch, partly because the sitting bird cannot cover all the eggs, and partly due to predation, mainly by jackals and hyenas. Young birds are precocial and can run immediately after hatching. They are cared for by the male and the dominant female for a considerable time. In the Nairobi National Park recently, the writer was fortunate to see on two occasions in one morning a hen with wings outstretched making continuous rushes towards his vehicle, creating a diversion while the male hastened the chicks away into the tall grass bordering the track on which the family had been caught.

The ostrich does not bury its head in the sand to make itself invisible. Various explanations have been given for this legend said to date back to the ancient Romans and Arabs. One is that the error may have stemmed from the sight of the bird almost touching the ground with its beak in search of small morsels of food. Another possibility may be the fact that the bird, when on the nest, occasionally sits flat and stretches out its neck along the ground in front to make itself less conspicuous.

At one time the ostrich was widespread over much of Africa and south-west Asia. Within the last two centuries it has become extinct in Asia and its range in Africa is considerably reduced. A typical example is the sad fate of the most northern representative, the Syrian race, formerly found in the desert country of Syria and Arabia. It is reported to have been fairly common there until 1914, but by 1941 had become extinct. Man with his precision rifles and fast cars must be held responsible for this extermination.

The soft plumage, caused by a lack of preen glands, and the attractiveness of the long black and white feathers have led to the use of ostrich feathers as decoration. In the early days the small quantity used was not serious, but when ostrich feathers became high fashion for women in the last century, the situation altered drastically. Fortunately, mainly for business reasons, ostrich farming was established as a means of obtaining a regular supply of feathers so the ostrich survived.

These farms began to appear in Cape Province in South Africa in the mid-1850s. To begin with the Southern Ostrich was used, but later it was crossed with other sub-species to increase the yield of feathers. At the turn of the century it was one of the largest businesses in that country, well over half a million birds being farmed in captivity. The demand for feathers has decreased greatly during this century with a consequent drop in price. Yet ostrich farming still remains a profitable business even though the number of birds kept in captivity is reduced to below 50,000. Ostrich skin is also used nowadays to make wallets and handbags to augment the income from the feathers.

Large tracts of veldt in South Africa, many hundreds of acres, are fenced off and the birds run freely in the huge enclosures to forage for their natural food. This is supplemented by green vegetation, such as lucerne, specially grown for the purpose. The feathers are cut, not plucked, at regular intervals. Increased production is achieved by removing a quantity of eggs from the nest for artificial incubation. This stimulates the hens to continue to lay more eggs than they normally would.

The various national reserves and parks throughout Africa provide sanctuary for the ostrich to live in the wild. The Masai and Somali Ostrich continue to thrive and for the time being the survival of the species seems to be assured.

2 Pelicans

Pelicans belong to the order Pelecaniformes, which is made up of aquatic birds whose main diet is fish, and which are characterized by having all four toes connected by a web. The family Pelecanidae consists of seven species under one genus and is widely distributed in tropical and some temperate parts of the world. Pelicans inhabit mainly inland waters, but some species are found in sheltered waters along the coast.

They are among the largest of birds, their length ranging from 50 to 70 inches. On land a pelican appears rather clumsy with its big ungainly body and stubby tail, balanced on short thick legs and strong feet. Its most characteristic feature is the very large bill, which is long and straight with a hook at the end. The upper mandible acts as a flat lid to the lower mandible from which is suspended the large, distensible gular pouch. This is not used for storage but as a scoop; as soon as the two to three gallons of water it takes in are drained away, the fish is swallowed. In appearance the various species show some differences such as the presence of a crest or a salmon pink suffusion during breeding, but in a majority of them the adult plumage is mainly white and the primaries are dark. The sexes are alike.

Although a great deal of flapping of the wings is required when taking off from water, pelicans are strong fliers once airborne and with their large broad wings (having a span of 120 inches in some species) can soar to great heights. They fly regularly in formation and a sight not easily forgotten is that of seeing them using thermals to climb higher and higher, the white plumage apparently changing suddenly to black as they wheel in unison.

Their main diet is fish and their gregarious nature is responsible for their rather peculiar method of catching prey. A number of birds arrange themselves in the water in a semi-circle, and gradually encircle or alternatively sweep the fish towards the shore, using vigorous flapping of the wings to 'beat' the fish forward into shallower water where they at last scoop them up, their heads dipping in the water in unison, a scene very reminiscent of the performance of a corps de ballet. Pelicans are mainly silent making only occasional croaking sounds, but nestlings may set up a noisy chatter.

White Pelican *Pelecanus onocrotalus*

Of the two species which occur in East Africa, the locally resident White Pelican is often augumented by migrants from Europe and Asia, but those that breed seem to be permanent residents. It is a large bird over 60 inches long. The adult is almost entirely white with black flight feathers. A number of changes take place in both sexes during breeding, the most distinctive being the development of a knob on the forehead. The male's plumage becomes a deep-salmon pink in colour and the bare skin of the face turns pinkish-yellow, this area being bright orange in the female. Thus identification of the two sexes during this period becomes easy. Breeding commences at the age of three to four years.

The birds nest in vast colonies and may build their nests in trees, occasionally in bushes, or even on the ground when no suitable sites above ground level are available. In Africa the main colonies lie along the chain of the Rift Valley Lakes, the largest probably being at Lake Rukwa with up to 40,000 pairs. Ground nests, built on almost bare rock, are particularly vulnerable to predation and the shy and sensitive birds readily desert their nests at the egg stage if disturbed by humans. Therefore the inaccessibility of the nesting colony is a significant factor in its success.

Considerable study of the breeding of the White Pelican has been carried out by Dr. Leslie H. Brown and his associates at Lake Shala in Ethiopia and Lake Elmenteita in Kenya. No record exists of its breeding in Kenya prior to 1968. This could be accounted for by the fact that the food supply in the Rift Valley lakes near Elmenteita was inadequate for the enormous needs of a breeding colony. These huge birds eat a prodigious amount, it being estimated that an adult requires four pounds of fish per day.

Above The flexible gular pouch and wide gape enable the pelican to take in a large fish, which is swallowed whole once the water has drained away.
Top Pelicans are strong and graceful fliers and this bird shows the huge wingspan as it glides in a thermal.

Below, left to right With much effort and flapping of wings, a White Pelican takes to the air in search of a better feeding ground.
Right Pelicans flying in formation.
Far right, top and centre The extraordinary contortions of the Pink-backed Pelicans preening.

In 1960 the health authorities introduced into Lake Nakuru the small alkali-tolerant fish *Tilapia grahami* to combat the breeding of mosquitoes around the lake shore. The little fish multiplied enormously and soon colonized the whole lake, and since 1961 Lake Nakuru has supported a large resident population of many species of fish-eating birds, including the White Pelican, which are estimated to harvest about 2,500 tons of *Tilapia grahami* from the lake every year. Nakuru has become the favourite feeding area of the White Pelican, whose numbers average about 3000 and once reached as high as 35,000.

At Elmenteita in 1968, nesting was triggered by the presence of Greater Flamingo colonies. This took place continuously from 1968 to 1971 during which period 7,000 to 8,000 pairs of pelicans bred successfully. In the severe competition for nesting places on the scattered sites on the lake, the much larger and heavier pelicans caused the flamingos to desert and the pelicans themselves ceased breeding abruptly in 1971, eggs and young of various ages being abandoned for no apparent reason, an abundant supply of food being still available. They returned in September 1973 and again in 1975.

No elaborate displays take place during courting or prior to mating. The average clutch is two eggs and rarely three. Both sexes incubate in turn and the naked, pink and helpless chicks are born after thirty to thirty-five days. They require continuous brooding at this stage, but after about three days begin to grow a dark brown down. During the first two weeks the young are fed on regurgitated liquid, later on fish brought by both parents.

The young leave the nests at this stage and form groups giving the impression that chicks are then fed indiscriminately by the adults; but this is not the case. Initially the parents seek out their young and later young birds are able to recognize their parents, whom they importune vigorously. At about eight weeks the feathered youngsters begin to swim and learn to fish, though still being fed by adults at this stage. At about ten weeks the young learn to fly and are then independent. The White Pelican is found throughout the Ethiopian Region on large areas on inland waters and rarely along the coast.

Pink-backed Pelican *Pelecanus rufescens*
This species is distinguished from the White Pelican, with whom it often shares a flock, by its smaller size (54 inches), pale grey plumage and large crest. It is a resident of Africa throughout the Ethiopian Region, and resembles the White Pelican in many of its habits.

Plate 4 White Pelicans *Pelecanus onocrotalus*. Cumbersome when taking off, these birds are majestic once airborne.

Plate 5 Pink-backed Pelicans *Pelecanus rufescens* gliding across the sparkling surface of the lake.

3 Cormorants

The cormorant family Phalacrocoracidae consists of about thirty species divided between two or three genera and thus has more species than all the other Pelecaniformes put together. The members are distributed over most of the world, some confined exclusively to coastal waters, others largely restricted to inland lakes and rivers, and some are found in both habitats.

Cormorants are medium to large in size, from 19 to 37 inches. The sexes are alike, with predominantly dark plumage, long necks and bodies, and are equally well adapted for swimming and flying. The bill, which is rather slender and has a hook at the end, is activated by strong muscles in the neck and head, necessary to hold fish when caught. They are mostly silent, except for gutteral sounds made at the nest.

Their short legs, as in other aquatic birds, are set far back, and propulsion under water is provided by their simultaneous backward movement. Wings are not used for this purpose. Because of the smallness of the air spaces in their bones, they swim rather low in the water and are very efficient hunters. Individuals account for about two pounds of fish per day and they spend little time in obtaining their daily needs, the rest of the day being spent in preening, resting and displaying.

Although they may catch crustaceans and amphibians, their main food consists of fish, which are caught, after underwater pursuit, with their hooked bills. A transparent nictitating membrane covers the eye during diving to enable the bird to see under water. The dives may be shallow or deep; the catch, particularly if big, is brought to the surface, tossed in the air, caught and swallowed head first.

It is a common sight to see cormorants perched on trees or rocks with their wings extended, and it is generally believed that they are drying out their water-logged plumage. Some authorities maintain, however, that 'once out of water the birds have no difficulty in shaking water drops off their plumage, for the individual feathers have become water repellant through the application of preen gland oil.' (Van Tets, 1968). Certain drying must take place, but the time on the perch is also used to digest the catch, the consequent reduction in weight enabling the bird both to take off and to fly easily. If disturbed during the digestive period, the stomach contents are regurgitated. Cormorants are powerful fliers, moving as much as sixty miles daily from their roosts to their feeding sites. They fly steadily with regular wing beats and short glides, not far above the surface if flying over water.

Most cormorants breed colonially, nests being built on rocks, trees or cliffs wherever suitable sites are available. Their nests of sticks or other materials are elaborate structures which are continually added to throughout the breeding cycle. The size of the usual clutch is two to four eggs, which have a chalky coating, and both parents take part in incubation, feeding and brooding the young.

White-necked Cormorant *Phalacrocorax carbo*

This is a member of the most widely distributed species with many races, and is a large bird about 36 inches long. Both sexes are alike in appearance, being blue-black in colour with white cheeks and throat. The underside of the neck is also white and this often extends to the breast.

Breeding starts between three and five years. They nest frequently in large colonies, on trees and bushes in suitable sites and their nests on partially submerged dead trees are a familiar site at Lake Naivasha in Kenya. A typical nest of sticks with a lining of vegetation or feathers is built and may contain two to four pale greenish-blue eggs with a chalky white outside layer. The incubation period is about thirty days and although the young are able to fly at about seven weeks, they do not leave the family until they are about twelve weeks old.

In East Africa, this species is confined exclusively to inland waters and is found in abundant quantities on Lakes Victoria and Turkana.

Long-tailed Cormorant *Phalacrocorax africanus*

The sexes are once again alike and the bird is distinguished from the White-necked Cormorant by being smaller in size (24 inches) and having entirely black underparts and a somewhat longer tail. They breed mostly in small colonies, the nest being constructed of sticks, reeds or seaweed in a suitable location near water. The two to four eggs are pale blue in colour with a chalky white covering.

The Long-tailed Cormorant is found on the coast as well as on inland lakes and rivers. Lakes in Uganda and Tanzania and Lake Turkana in Kenya provide a favourite habitation for this species.

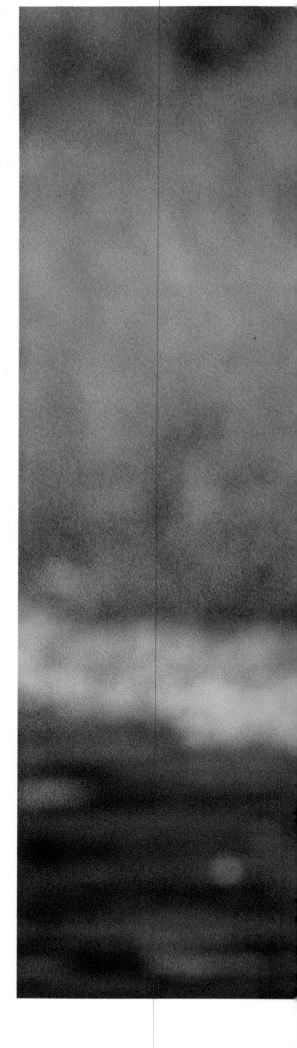

Above White-necked Cormorants nest and roost on a group of dead thorn trees in Lake Nakuru National Park.
Above left Dead trees in Lake Naivasha provide rather over-crowded nesting sites for these cormorants.
Left Cormorants are often seen drying their wings after diving, as their feathers are inadequately waterproofed. This is a Long-tailed Cormorant.

Page 31, Plate 6 A Long-tailed Cormorant *Phalacrocorax africanus* perched on a stump on the bank of a river in Uganda.

Previous page, Plate 7 A sociable cluster of White-necked Cormorants *Phalacrocorax carbo* drying their wings in the early morning sun.

4 Darters

Darters are so similar in general habits to the cormorants that some authorities classify them under Phalacrocoracidae, the family of the latter, but they must be considered as a separate family because of certain structural peculiarities. The darter, unlike the cormorant, has a long, straight and pointed bill, which is not hooked. The long neck, which when at rest assumes an S-shape, has a peculiar articulation of the vertebrae that enables the bird to shoot its bill forward as if triggered which facilitates its special method of catching fish.

The family Anhingidae has a number of forms, variously grouped under one to four species, but only one genus, and their world-wide distribution is confined to tropical and sub-tropical areas. The darter is exclusively a freshwater bird frequenting lakes, swamps and rivers, where fishing is suitable, and even sheltered bays and mouths of rivers along the coast. It swims very low in the water, with only the long neck and head showing above the surface like a swimming snake, hence the name snake bird.

The darter lives on fish and other aquatic animals and whilst preying can stay under water for several minutes where it swims slowly with wings partly open. Its catch is sometimes speared and impaled on the bill and at other times caught between the mandibles. The stunned or dead fish is brought to the surface, tossed up in the air, caught and swallowed head first. Having heavy bones with small air spaces, darters can dive and submerge effortlessly and silently; but because of the permeability of their plumage they spend little time in the water, unless fishing or escaping from terrestrial enemies. Most of the time they perch upright on branches over water or on half submerged logs with their wings open.

Darters have great difficulty in taking off from the surface of the water, flapping their wings vigorously in the process, but once airborne they are remarkably efficient fliers. Like the pelicans they use thermal air currents to soar upwards in spirals and then glide downwards with neck extended and wings and tail feathers spread, into the next thermal.

A bulky nest of sticks is generally built on trees in water or on overhanging branches. An established colony may consist of up to a hundred nests in close proximity, often communally with cormorants, spoonbills, ibises and herons. The male selects a nest site and defends it against intruders until a female persuades him to accept her. The female builds the nest with material provided by the male, and both share nest-guarding duties.

Three to six pale bluish or greenish eggs with an outer chalky covering are laid, at intervals of forty-eight hours or more and the consequent disparity in the ages of the chicks causes a certain amount of domination of the younger by the older nestlings. The newly hatched birds, after an incubation of about thirty days, are naked and blind but acquire a white down in a few days. They are well feathered at four weeks and independent at six to eight weeks, depending on how well they have been fed.

African Darter *Anhinga rufa*
This is the only species occurring in East Africa. It looks like an elongated cormorant with its length of about 38 inches consisting mainly of the pointed bill, S-shaped neck and the long stiff tail rounded at the end. In the adult male, the head and back of the neck are chestnut and black and the remainder of the neck is chestnut, with a white stripe running from the gape along part of each side. The underparts are black. The bird is usually silent except for the low croaking sound it makes at the nest.

Left When feeding, the young darter inserts its head right inside the mouth of its parent.

35

Plate 8 An African Darter *Anhinga rufa* in a
typical pose, spreading its large wings to dry.

5 Herons and Egrets

Herons and egrets belong to the family Ardeidae of the order Ciconiiformes. This order has about 118 species, which are distinguished from others which live in and around water, by almost always having characteristically graceful long legs and elongated bills, adapted for wading and fishing in shallow water. About sixty-two species, which make up the family of herons, egrets and bitterns, are distributed mostly over tropical and sub-tropical areas of the world and are well represented in East Africa by some eighteen species. Of these, the Grey and Purple Herons are both residents and migrants and one bitterns is a visitor from Europe during the non-breeding season. Almost all members of the family are found in the vicinity of water, inland near rivers, swamps and lakes and along the coast in sheltered bays.

Herons are medium to large in size but, with a few exceptions, most of this is accounted for by the long neck and the straight, pointed and elongated bill which is attached to a slim body on moderate to long legs. All four toes are also long and slender, and have no webs. The wings are broad and the flight is strong even though it may appear clumsy because of its deliberateness. In flight the legs are extended behind and the neck retracted into an S-shape, thus distinguishing this family from spoonbills, cranes and storks, which fly with their necks extended.

The food of most of the species consists predominantly of fish, but frogs, insects and small mammals also form part of their diet, the prey being swallowed whole and undigested material being regurgitated in the form of pellets. When searching for food the bird may wade, walk slowly or make rapid dashes from side to side, but most characteristically, the heron stands motionless with its neck usually retracted, waiting for the prey to come within striking distance. The special structure of the cervical vertebrae permits it to thrust its head forward very rapidly and the prey is either grasped or, more rarely, speared by the pointed bill. Mention should be made of the use of wings by the Black Heron *Egretta ardesiaca* to help in its quest for food. The head is bent forward, with the bill pointing downwards, the wings opened and brought rapidly forward over the head so that the tips of the feathers are nearly touching the water, thus forming an 'umbrella'. It is believed that fish wander under the canopy to take refuge. Another possible reason for this device is that it enables the bird to see better under water as bright surface reflections are cut out. Whatever the explanation, the sight of a number of Black Herons fishing at Lake Jipe in Tsavo West National Park in Kenya is not to be easily forgotten.

The sexes do not show any conspicuous difference in their plumage, which is loose in texture, even during the breeding season when they develop long, decorative plumes on the head, back, breast or neck. Instead of preening their feathers with preen oil, herons make

Below A flash of white as a flock of Cattle Egrets takes off from the shore of Lake Jipe.

characteristic use of powder down, which occurs in patches on the breast and rump and, in some species, in the groin area. Powder down consists of feathers which grow continuously from the base and do not moult. The tips of the feathers disintegrate gradually forming a powder which the birds use to clean their plumage of fish remains and grease. Beaks and claws are used, the claw of the middle toe having a special serrated edge.

Most herons and egrets are gregarious in the breeding season, nesting in colonies and indeed some of them remain social even when not breeding, flocking together for flight, or roosting communally in trees. Platform nests of sticks are built in trees, shrubs, reeds and even on rocks when other suitable sites are not available. Elaborate courtship and sexual displays are performed in the air and at the nest, which is usually built by both parents. Clutches of two to five eggs are laid, which they incubate in turn. Food is brought in the stomach and regurgitated directly into the beak of the young in the early days, and later, onto the edge of the nest. Most of this species make harsh croaks and squawks.

Squacco Heron *Ardeola ralloides*

This is a rather thickset heron of about 18 inches with rich biscuit colour plumage and white wings, rump, tail and belly, which become strikingly apparent when the bird is flying. Otherwise it is very inconspicuous and blends completely with its surroundings.

It is a gregarious breeder, not only with its own species, but forming colonies with other small herons and egrets and nests among reeds, dry bushes or sometimes on low trees. The normal clutch is of two or three eggs which are greenish-blue in colour, but little study seems to have been done of its breeding behaviour. The Squacco Heron is common in the whole of Africa and, like the Cattle Egret, it frequents swamps, marshes and lakes showing particular preference for a thick cover of water plants.

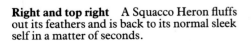

Right and top right A Squacco Heron fluffs out its feathers and is back to its normal sleek self in a matter of seconds.

Above and top The Black-headed Heron can be seen gazing about with great concentration, as it hunts for food both in water and on dry land.

Plate 9 This proud bird, the Goliath Heron *Ardea goliath*, is the largest of all the herons.

Plate 10 The alert gaze of the Squacco Heron *Ardeola ralloides* as it waits for possible prey.

Overleaf, top left Cooling itself at the water's edge, this wild buffalo is unperturbed by its attendant Cattle Egret.
Left to right A Black Heron demonstrates its typical 'umbrella' method of hunting for prey. Unsuspecting fish will wander under the canopy of its wings.
Bottom, Plate 11 Cattle Egret *Bubulcus ibis*. These birds feed on insects disturbed by the larger mammals as they graze.

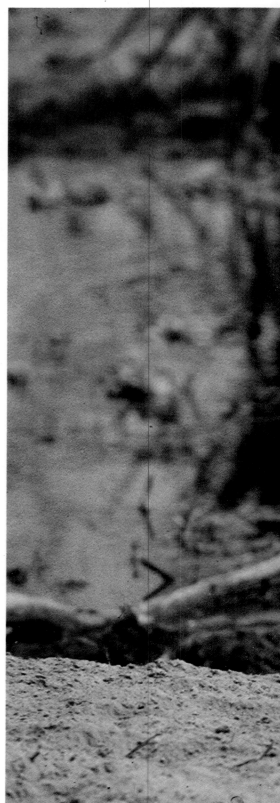

Cattle Egret *Bubulcus ibis*

This is also known as the Buff-backed Heron, but this name can lead to confusion as the bird, unlike the Squacco Heron, has pale buff plumage on its upper parts only during the breeding season, being white the rest of the time. It is about 20 inches long, with short legs and yellow bill and can be distinguished from the Little Egret as it is more thickset.

The expansion of its range from the Old World to the New in the last thirty to forty years is an astounding success story in these times when most other populations are on the decline. The Cattle Egret originally accompanied herds of large wild mammals, as it still does in East Africa, but it can also be seen in sizable flocks walking amongst domestic animals as they graze, feeding on the insects disturbed by their movement. They are also known to feed on blood-sucking parasites of the larger mammals and are therefore welcomed by farmers for the protection from pests which they provide for their livestock.

The introduction of domestic cattle in large numbers with the consequent opening up of new areas of grassland by modern stock-farming methods provided the necessary ecological niche, and the Cattle Egret population expanded explosively, so much so that after enlarging its African range in all directions, it was forced to look for 'pastures new'. It crossed the Atlantic in a westward direction, colonizing the West Indies and South America in the 1930s, and had established itself in North America by the early 1950s. By 1948 it had also travelled east to Australia, where it joined others already introduced artificially as a beneficial species. Under the favourable conditions in these continents, with their abundant and hitherto unexploited food supply, the Cattle Egret continues to multiply.

They are communal birds both in and out of the breeding season. After a day of feeding amongst grazing cattle they can be seen to congregate and fly in flocks to their roosting sites, which may be some distance away, providing an unforgettable sight of flashing white wings in simultaneous flight against the darkening sky. Nesting colonies are built either on their own or in association with other herons, such as the Squacco and Little Egrets, usually near water, in dense reed beds or other marshy sites. Congregation and close density of birds seems to be a significant factor in providing the necessary stimulus for breeding, sufficient rain being a prerequisite for its success. One to three eggs are laid at intervals of forty-eight hours, incubation by both sexes starting with the first egg, which hatches after three to four weeks. The parents protect their young tenderly, providing shade with their wings during the hot part of the day. Cattle Egrets are common throughout the Ethiopian Region and frequent swamps, pasture lands, lake margins and, rarely, the coast.

Green-backed Heron *Butorides striatus*

This is related to the Green Heron *Butorides virescens* of sub-tropical North and Middle America. It is a small, compact, short-legged bird (16 inches) with greenish upper parts and paler grey below. This bird is shy and largely nocturnal, spending most of its time under deep cover in swamps, wooded river banks and coastal mangrove swamps. It is a solitary nester, building a concealed nest near water.

Black-headed Heron *Ardea melanocephala*

This is a medium-sized heron about 38 inches in length and is distinguished from the Grey or Common Heron *Ardea cinerea*, to which it is closely related, by its black crown, neck and grey underparts. Both herons eat fish but the Black-headed Heron is equally happy to feed on insects, frogs and small rodents, which it often hunts quite a distance away from water.

Plate 12 Hunched on its perch, this
Green-backed Heron *Butorides striatus*, is a
shy, nocturnal bird.

Left, Plate 13 A Black-headed Heron *Ardea melanocephala* stalking amongst the reeds in search of prey.
Below left, right and bottom Having caught a fish in Lake Naivasha, this Goliath Heron was mobbed by various birds, in the hope that it would drop its catch. The heron thus reacted sharply, raising its 'hackles', when a pelican approached soon afterwards.

It can be seen frequently on dry land standing quite still, gazing intently at its prey and then moving its head from side to side with increasing rapidity before darting it forward to catch its victim.

It is common in East Africa on inland waters and the coast, but also likes to breed in villages and towns. In Kampala, Uganda, there is a large heronry in the grounds of Makerere College and in Nairobi, Kenya, the Black-headed Heron has nested for many years in the stores yard of the railway station. Ornithologists M. E. W. North and L. H. Brown have studied this colony over the years and according to the former it was first established in 1954. The typical large nests of sticks are built on tall eucalyptus trees and nesting is practically continuous throughout the year provided the rains are suitable, the peak of activity being reached during the long rains in April and May. Two blue or greenish-blue eggs are laid, the incubation period is about twenty-five days and the young leave the nest for good after being fully fledged at approximately sixty days.

Goliath Heron *Ardea goliath*

This bird has the distinction of being the largest of all herons, its length being nearly 60 inches. With its grey and chestnut plumage it is easily distinguished from the similarly coloured Purple Heron *Ardea purpurea* by the difference in their sizes, the latter being nearer 36 inches. Since its diet consists almost exclusively of fish, it can be regarded as a true shore bird, frequenting areas of coastal and inland waters, where it can be seen standing in shallow water looking for prey. Because of its size, it can wade deeper and catch bigger fish and therefore does not compete with other herons; but other birds are known to mob it, endeavouring to make it drop its catch.

Goliath Herons occur singly or in pairs in limited numbers from Senegal and Egypt to South Africa and their nests are not built in colonies, presumably because they are large enough to defend themselves. The nest is a large platform of sticks and reeds, about three feet in diameter, built close to water either on low bushes, reed beds or other vegetation. Two to three chalky blue eggs are laid which hatch in about thirty-two days.

6 Storks

Eight out of the seventeen species of storks (Family Ciconiidae) are to be found in Africa and two of them, the White and the Black Storks, are Palaearctic migrants. They are all large, heavily-built birds with long necks, very long legs and stout, pointed, extensive bills which may be straight, up-curved or down-curved. Some species are bare-faced while in some others the whole of the head and upper neck are practically without feathers. The sexes are alike in appearance.

With their long, broad wings they are efficient and strong fliers, and fly with the neck extended and the legs trailing behind. Some species migrate over short distances whilst others travel very far, so their ability to soar is not only an advantage but a necessity.

Storks are generally gregarious and can often be seen on open plains and fields hunting for their favourite diet of grasshoppers and locusts. Some are seen near water, where their diet may consist of fish, amphibians and molluscs; a few are carrion eaters. They mostly nest colonially in trees, where large nests of sticks are built in the form of a platform, often very high up, in which are laid three to six whitish eggs. Both parents build the nest, incubate the eggs and care for the young. Elaborate courting and greeting rituals take place, which have been well studied in the White Stork.

Perhaps the Marabou *Leptoptilos crumeniferus* is the most common stork in Africa, where, because of its scavenging habits, it is associated with towns and villages. Between 1964 and 1967 extensive studies were carried out at the small breeding colony at Kitale, Kenya by Philip Kahl. According to him (1968) 'most nesting colonies are located near a dual source of food: (1) a supply of carrion to form the bulk of the diet and (2) a source of fish, frogs or other small vertebrates to fulfil the calcium requirements of the growing young'.

Away from human habitation, these storks are often found in association with vultures. A kill in any of the National Parks is readily located by the presence of vultures in the area, both on the wing and on the ground. Immediately the carcass has been deserted by the killer, the vultures move in on it in large numbers and with them come the Marabou. With their considerable size and strong bills they readily intimidate the vultures, who make way for them. These huge birds are extremely ugly, with their pendular gular sacs.

A brief mention may be made of the small Open-billed Stork *Anastomus lamelligerus* with its specially adapted bill. This has a large gap between the base and the tip, like the opening in a nut-cracker, which enables the bird to crack the shells of molluscs and snails.

During the European winter, subject to feeding conditions being satisfactory, the White

Left   This clearly shows the nut-cracker-like opening in the beak of an Open-billed Stork which enables it to crack the shells of molluscs and snails.
Right   This Abdim's Stork *Ciconia abdimii* spreads its wings in the sunshine on the shore of Lake Jipe.
Far right   Great numbers of White Storks come to the Ethiopian Region in the winter. This one follows a plough in the hope of finding food.

Stork *Ciconia ciconia* is to be found in flocks in many parts of East Africa, particularly the Rift Valley, where it is often seen on the grassy plains. The departure of these birds from their breeding areas is a classical story of migration, which it has been possible to study in great depth because of the birds' close association during, nesting, with human habitations.

The migration of the White Storks is a very impressive event, noticed even in biblical times. They are superb fliers travelling straight with a minimum flapping of wings; but to allow them to soar, they need thermals, which are columns of rising hot air created by the sun on suitable terrain. The birds discover these columns, in which they rise higher and higher until they are mere dots in the sky, then glide in the selected direction, losing altitude until they find the next thermal, when the process is repeated. Because there are no thermals over water they confine their flights over this feature of the earth's surface to a minimum, which accounts for the concentration of a large number of White Storks at the shortest crossing points to Africa.

They leave Europe by two main routes, which seem to diverge somewhere in Northern Europe, at either end of the Mediterranean. One passage is over the Straits of Gibraltar from where the birds arrive in North Africa and surrounding areas. The second major crossing is at the narrowest part of the Bosphorus and down the Jordan Valley, reaching the Nile at Wadi Halfa. From here the birds spread southwards into East Africa.

Yellow-billed Stork *Mycteria ibis*

Sometimes also known, incorrectly, as the Wood Ibis, this stork is about 42 inches long, has black and pinkish-white plumage, (the latter acquiring a crimson tinge during the breeding season), red legs, a bare face and a slightly down-curved orange bill.

Its main diet is fish and the bird is seen most commonly on inland waters, rarely at the coast, throughout East Africa. It has been observed occasionally to open and raise one wing whilst fishing, but the exact reason for this practice is not known. It could well be a technique to help locate fish under water by cutting out surface reflections in the shadow of the wing, as in the case of the Black Heron, or to maintain its balance.

Saddle-billed Stork *Ephippiorhynchus senegalensis*

This is a large, handsome bird over 60 inches long, with black and white plumage and a red bill, which has a black band round its middle. There is also a patch of yellow at the base of the upper mandible.

The bird is widely distributed throughout most of the Ethiopian Region but nowhere in large numbers. It frequents marshes, swamps and edges of inland water and is solitary in habit, though sometimes seen in pairs.

Overleaf left, Plate 14 With its distinctive bill, the Yellow-billed Stork *Mycteria ibis* is a familiar bird, found wherever there is water.
Overleaf right, Plate 15 A Saddle-billed Stork *Epippiorhyncus senegalensis* stepping delicately through the water.

51

7 Ibises and Spoonbills

The family Threskiornithidae is represented in Africa by two sub-families: ibises which consist of four species, one of which, the Glossy Ibis *Plegadis falcinellus*, having a resident form identical with the Palaearctic migrant; and the spoonbills represented by two species, the African and the European Spoonbills, the latter being a rare winter visitor from the north. Despite the fact that spoonbills, with their flattened spatulate bills, look so different from ibises with their thin, long and down-curved bills, they are classified in the same family. This is because of similarities between the young of the two families. Both have narrow, pointed bills, which in the case of spoonbills, become flattened horizontally and widened at the tip only at the adult stage.

Ibises are moderate-sized birds varying in length from 20 to 30 inches. Their most distinctive feature is the long, thin, down-curved bill which they use for probing in mud and soil to capture their prey. In some species the face only is bare of feathers and in others the bareness extends to the head and the neck. The exposed skin may be either black or brightly coloured. Plumage shows a colour range from white to dark, the latter often with a metallic sheen, and one South American species, the Scarlet Ibis *Eudocimus ruber*, is brilliant red when fully adult. The sexes are almost alike. Ibises generally fly in flocks with their necks and heads fully extended forward; their regular wing beats alternate with short spells of gliding, thus differing from the flight of the spoonbills which do not glide.

They are well distributed over all warm and tropical areas and their most usual habitat is in the vicinity of fresh water, where they feed on crustaceans, worms, insects, reptiles and fish. Except for the Hadada Ibis, which has a loud raucous call, the ibises generally make little sound, apart from croaks during nesting. They are usually gregarious and most species nest colonially, building typical nests of sticks, with a cup-shaped cavity lined with grass, on trees, bushes, or reeds and even on rocks if no other suitable site is available. Two to four coloured eggs, sometimes with markings, are incubated by both parents, which also tend the young.

Sacred Ibis *Threskiornis aethiopica*

The ancient Egyptians regarded this ibis as sacred and were responsible for its popular name. The bird has been depicted on many murals and frequent mummified specimens have been discovered in tombs. It was revered as the embodiment if Thoth, the god of wisdom, the scribe of the gods and inventor of writing, who was depicted with the head of an ibis. But the Sacred Ibis has been extinct in Egypt for over a hundred years. With white plumage and dark ornamental feathers on the lower back, it is a striking-looking bird, 30 inches long. The head and neck are bare of feathers and the exposed skin is black.

The Sacred Ibis is communal in its habits and flocks can be seen, in V-formation, flying to their roosting area after a day of feeding elsewhere. The colony of nests, often with herons and egrets, may be built on trees, bushes or even on marshy ground. The two or three whitish eggs hatch in a little over twenty-one days and the young are fully fledged from five to six weeks. The nestlings have straight bills, which when first hatched, they insert into the beak of the feeding parent. When the chicks are older, the food is regurgitated into their mouths.

The Sacred Ibis is found throughout the Ethiopian Region, frequenting marshes, swamps, pasture land and flood plains.

Hadada Ibis *Bostrychia hagedash*

The loud piercing cry 'hah – hah – hah' of this ibis, and the calls of the Fish Eagle and the Crowned Crane are perhaps the bird sounds most typical of Africa. The Hadada Ibis is frequently heard at daybreak and sunset and even on bright moonlit nights as it flies between its roosting site and feeding area. It is about the same size as the Glossy Ibis, but its entire plumage is olive-brown, with pale underparts, head and neck and a metallic green sheen on the wing coverts.

It is a sociable bird, especially during the non-breeding season, when small flocks can be seen in flight, feeding or at roost; but, unlike other ibises, it is a solitary nester. Three or four greenish-buff eggs with brown spots are laid at irregular intervals, with the result that the fledglings are at different stages of development. The incubation period is about twenty-eight days and the young are ready to leave the nest at about five weeks.

The Hadada Ibis is common in East Africa, where it frequents swamps, marshes, edges of lakes and pasture land. Often seen near villages and towns, and in cultivated gardens, the birds are quite tame and, if disturbed, fly off at the last minute uttering their characteristic cry as an alarm call.

The loud, piercing call of this bird, the Hadada Ibis, is one of the most typical sounds of Africa.

Below left and bottom, Plates 16 and 18 The Sacred Ibises *Threskiornis aethiopica* owe their name to the ancient Egyptians who considered them to be sacred.
Below, Plate 17 The plumage of the Glossy Ibis *Plegadis falcinellus*, when caught in the right light, has a metallic sheen of purple, green and bronze.

Glossy Ibis *Plegadis falcinellus*

This is the only member of the species with an almost world-wide distribution and which still breeds in Europe. The breeding and resident African species is augmented by additional northern visitors. It is much smaller than the other ibises, being about 24 inches long and appears almost black, unless the right light conditions prevail when the plumage shows a metallic gloss of purple, green and bronze. Dark greenish-blue eggs, usually three to four, hatch in about three weeks and the young fledge at five to six weeks.

This species is gregarious and is found on most inland lakes and swamps from time to time, but numbers vary considerably from year to year.

Top left   Often seen in pairs, the Hadada Ibis are most sociable during the non-breeding season when they gather in small flocks to feed or roost.
Left   Believed to be divine by the ancient Egyptians, the Sacred Ibis represented Thoth, the god of wisdom.
Right   Despite its flattened, spatulate bill, the African Spoonbill *Platalea alba* is closely related to the ibises.
Overleaf, Plate 19   The noisy Hadada Ibis *Bostrychia hagedash* can be heard at sunrise and sunset, and on bright moonlit nights.

8 Flamingos

The family Phoenicopteridae consists of four species of flamingos, although some authorities divide them into six. In the latter case, the three races of the Greater Flamingo are regarded as separate species, but because of their similar bill structure, most taxonomists consider them as belonging to the species *Phoenicopterus ruber*.

It has been estimated by Brown (1973) that there are over 6½ million flamingos in the world. The Lesser Flamingo *Phoeniconaias minor* is the most numerous, there being about five times as many as all the rest of the species put together. Approximately 5½ million Lesser Flamingos are distributed over Africa, India and the Persian Gulf, the great majority, about 4 million, living on the more or less foul alkaline lakes, which form a chain in the floor of the Great Rift Valley in the East African territories of Kenya and Tanzania.

A fascinating bird, beautiful individually and breathtaking when appearing in large numbers, the flamingo is found in specialized habitats because of its feeding habits. It is invariably associated with brackish or salt-water lakes or lagoons, usually in warm climates and sometimes at high altitudes. It is a large bird 36 to 72 inches in length, the female being appreciably smaller than the male. It has long, usually red legs with webbed feet; a long sinuous neck; bare face and a large red bill. In adult plumage the bird is invariably pink and red, the upper wing coverts being particularly so, and has black flight feathers.

The unique feature of the flamingo is its bill, which is specially adapted for its highly individual style of food intake, which ensures that hardly any other bird competes with it for its nutritional source. The lower mandible is large and trough-like and the tongue lies in a groove in this. The upper mandible is small and fits on the lower one like a lid. A sharp downward curve of the bill near its centre ensures that, when feeding, the upper jaw faces downwards. The presence of lamellae which line the inside of the mouth cavity, combined with an edging of stiff excluder hairs convert this bill into a very efficient filtration mechanism. While feeding the flamingo moves its head from side to side and the water with its fine food particles (the coarser grains having been excluded by the stiff hairs) is sucked in by the retraction of the tongue's piston-like action. The water is then forced out by its forward movement, leaving the food particles trapped by the filtering lamellae. The food mass is worked on the tongue and then swallowed.

The three races of the Greater Flamingo have an additional filtering refinement: a shallow keel to their upper mandible and only part of the interior is covered with the hair-like lamellae, the other three species having a deep keel which fits snugly into the lower mandible and the entire inside surface is covered with fine lamellae. As a result of this adaptation, the Lesser Flamingos can feed on much smaller organisms and their diet consists almost exclusively of algae and diatoms. The Greater Flamingos, on the other hand, also feed on molluscs, crustaceae, and organic particles in mud, as well as some algae and diatoms. The filtration method of feeding does not help the flamingo to select its type of food, it only controls the size of the food particles taken in. This efficient feeding

mechanism means that the floating organisms are filtered out almost dry, thus preventing an intake of alkaline water in any quantity, which could otherwise prove lethal. Flamingos prefer to drink less saline water and regularly frequent springs or fresh water inlets to supply this need.

Flamingos are efficient swimmers and fly with ease, their long necks extended forward in flight. Considerable numbers, often at night, giving a loud honking call as they fly. These characteristics, amongst others, point to their close relationship to ducks and geese. By nature highly gregarious, they occur in large numbers, sometimes well over a million in one place, providing an unforgettable experience for the lucky observer. The distribution of flamingos must surely be influenced by the availability of their enormous food requirements, but why they come and go from their regular haunts, as they do, is still something of a mystery.

Nesting is colonial and very large numbers, over half a million, may be involved. Typical truncated, cone-shaped nests about 6 to 12 inches high are built of mud, with a shallow depression at the top scooped out by the bill. However, variations from the norm have been observed in the absence of suitable building material. A single chalky white egg is usual, but occasionally two are laid. Incubation is about sixty-five to seventy-five days. The grey-coloured young are able to swim at about ten days, but are dependent on the parents to feed them until the initial straight bill takes its characteristic shape and the filtering structure is properly formed. Observing the large groups of growing young wandering all over the nesting site attended by only a few adults, one might assume that the young are fed indiscriminately. But this is not the case. The parent calls and only its own young, recognizing the voice, runs towards it and is fed with food of liquid consistency regurgitated by the parent. And this continues until the fledgling's first flight. The immature birds moult into adult plumage at one to one and a half years, but do not breed for several years afterwards.

Left A flight of Lesser Flamingos. These unpredictable birds will gather to feed in their hundreds and then disappear as suddenly as they came.
Below Young flamingos are dwarfed by the head of an adult.

Left, Plate 20   Greater Flamingo
Phoenicopterus ruber. A mother gazes
protectively at her chick.
Below, Plate 21   A Lesser Flamingo
Phoeniconaias minor in flight stands out
against the green of the crater lake, inside an
extinct volcano.

The Greater and the Lesser Flamingo are the two species found in East Africa, of which the latter is a hundred times as numerous as the former. The alkaline lakes of the Great Rift Valley are their home, with Lakes Natron and Magadi being perhaps the harshest areas, with high concentration of sodium carbonate, covered with foul black mud in the case of Natron, and the less severe but still inhospitable Lakes Elmenteita, Nakuru and Bogoria. All these lakes support between them more flamingos than the rest of the world.

Greater Flamingo *Phoenicopterus ruber*

The three races of the Greater Flamingo which are present in Africa, Asia, Europe and North and South America number nearly one million. Of these about 40,000 occur in East Africa. The adult male is about 66 inches long and the female 6 inches shorter. Both sexes have white plumage with a pink wash, bright coral-red outer wing coverts, black flight feathers and a pink bill tipped black. The clutch is a single chalky white egg which is incubated in twenty-eight to thirty days and the fledging period is seventy-five days.

The Greater Flamingo occurs in feeding groups in association with the Lesser, and the difference in their feeding techniques and habits accounts for the ability of the small number of Greater Flamingo to co-exist with the overwhelmingly large number of the Lesser. Having a bill with a shallow keel and fewer lamellae, it can feed on large organisms such as crustaceans and small molluscs which it gathers from the bottom of the lake. Lesser Flamingos exist on microscopic particles which they collect from the top inch or so of the surface. Thus they are able to feed all over the lake, while the Greater Flamingo's feeding area is restricted, although it can stand and feed in deeper water. Therefore there is no competition between the two resident species.

When Brown (1973) first discovered from the air breeding colonies of Lesser Flamingo on Lake Natron in 1954, he also spotted several groups of the Greater nesting among them. An abortive attempt to reach these colonies on foot, which nearly cost him his life, made a close study of these nests situated on 'one of the foulest spots on earth' impossible, and it was not until the end of 1956, when the Greater Flamingo decided to nest at Lake Elmenteita, that he was able to undertake the work which has made him the acknowledged authority in this field. His book 'The Mystery of the Flamingos' first published in 1959 and revised in 1973 is a mine of information, besides being a spellbinding narrative of fascinating exploration and adventure; regular observations were made from 1956 onwards

by Brown and his associates at Lake Elmenteita.

Greater Flamingos breed irregularly, and mainly use two areas in East Africa for this purpose. The colonies on Lake Natron in Tanzania, where they generally breed in association with the Lesser Flamingo and where they build atypical mud nests on soda flats, are more significant because of their regularity and success. Breeding at Lake Elmenteita has had some importance in recent years although since 1968, its success has been minimal for reasons to be explained later. Even at this site, if mud is present, the usual type of nest is built, its height decreasing the further it is situated from the source of mud supply; but since the islets on which the colonies are established consist of black lava rocks with little vegetation, atypical nests built of pebbles on bare rocks, sometimes lined with feathers or vegetation are also present.

Even during 1956, the first year of observation, Brown (1973) was able to discover the major factor in the lowering of breeding success and the Marabou Stork was the culprit. A handful of these birds, by climbing on to the islets where the flamingos were sitting on eggs almost ready to hatch, caused the parents to desert in large numbers. No apparent aggression took place, but the flamingos, being naturally gregarious, disliked being isolated from their fellows and when some left in fright, others followed suit causing a mass exodus.

By 1968, another factor had made its appearance. White Pelicans, which had never bred in Kenya before this date, started nesting at Elmenteita. At Lake Nakuru the abundant supply of food, in this case the fish *Tilapia grahami*, necessary for a large nesting colony,

Below Large groups of growing young, wandering amongst a few adults, may give the impression that they are fed indiscriminately, but this is not so.
Far right, top to bottom Near the water at Lake Elmenteita, a typical nest is built, whereas further inland, the egg may be laid on bare stones, or in a hollow lined with a little foliage.
Below right This young Greater Flamingo seems to be lost amidst the towering forest of legs.

was of significance; but the actual breeding of the pelicans at Elmenteita was triggered by the presence of flamingo breeding colonies, and 7000 to 8000 pairs bred there successfully and continuously from 1968 to 1971. Severe competition for nesting places took place on the scattered sites; the larger and heavier pelicans forced the flamingos to leave and so effectively prevented their breeding.

Unidentified disease, as a result of which about 3000 chicks were lost in 1966, seems to have played no part in other years. It may be mentioned that human interference and predators other than Marabou had only a minor effect. A combination of all the above factors reduced the breeding during 1969 to 1971 to practically nothing. The pelicans left abruptly in 1971 for no apparent reason and did not return until late 1973. The Greater Flamingo did not return to breed at Elmenteita after the unexplained departure of the pelicans, and have not until the present time (March 1976).

Lesser Flamingo *Phoeniconaias minor*
Although also found in India and the Persian Gulf, four million Lesser Flamingo, of the total world population of 5½ million, have their stronghold in East Africa. This is the smallest of all flamingos and its size of 36 inches is almost half that of the Greater. It is also much brighter pink and has a deep carmine-red bill. The single white egg hatches at twenty-eight to thirty days and the chicks, provided food supplies are adequate, fledge between sixty-five and seventy days.

The Lesser Flamingo is frequently present in large numbers, often well exceeding a million, on the alkaline lakes of the Rift Valley and is responsible for a fantastic spectacle impossible to describe in words. The far fewer Greater Flamingos, outnumbered by nearly a hundred to one, stalk amongst them, easily spotted by their spectacular height. The Lesser Flamingos feed almost exclusively on the microscopic blue-green algae and diatoms suspended near the water surface, while the Greater obtain their nourishment from the bottom of the lake.

As can be imagined, a staggering amount of nourishment is taken out of the waters of the alkaline lakes by these astronomical numbers. According to Brown (1973) the intake of food of a million Lesser Flamingos is 180 tons daily or 5400 tons in a year! This works out at an annual intake of eight tons per acre of one million birds at Lake Nakuru, assuming that, under normal conditions, its total surface area is about 8500 acres. And this may be considered typical of the other soda lakes in the Rift.

It is clear that an abundant supply of algae, especially the blue-green algae *Spirulina platensis*, is essential to the well-being of the Lesser Flamingo. Research work has been carried out over a number of years and the opinion is that conductivity and alkalinity, due to the high concentration of carbonates, combined with relatively warm temperatures, the droppings of millions of birds and sunlight provide optimum conditions for their profuse growth. It seems reasonable to assume that the rise or fall in the lake level caused by weather conditions influences the concentration of salts present, which in turn affects the production of the blue-green algae but this has not yet been confirmed scientifically. The Nakuru Wildlife Trust, established in 1971 at Lake Nakuru, continues to study the ecology of the Rift Valley Lakes.

An adequate supply of food, however, does not seem to be the only factor influencing the presence or absence of flamingos. Enormous fluctuations in numbers take place on these lakes, birds leaving a particular lake even when the amount of blue-green algae present in it is quite evident. That its presence or absence is of significance is borne out by recent events at Lake Nakuru.

The main and perhaps the only regular breeding ground of the Lesser Flamingo in East Africa was discovered by L. H. Brown in 1954 to be at Lake Natron. This discovery was the culmination of his continuous efforts over a number of years to find their breeding sites. Between 100,000 and 150,000 nesting pairs of Lesser Flamingo were seen from the air. The inaccessibility of the breeding area, situated in the middle of this inhospitable lake, largely dry with crystalline carbonate deposits overlying foul black mud, made a close study of the breeding colonies impossible, and it was not until 1962, when due to abnormal weather conditions, Lesser Flamingo bred at the more easily approached Lake Magadi that Brown, with his co-workers, was able to complete his observations. It was noted that the breeding behaviour of the Lesser Flamingo closely paralleled that of the Greater.

Previous page, Plate 22 A crowded scene at the breeding ground of the Greater Flamingos *Phoenicopterus ruber*.
Below Lesser Flamingos congregate in large numbers at Crater Lake B on Central Island in Lake Turkana.

9 Ducks and Geese

The family Anatidae (Anseriformes) is made up of many species, which show a very wide variety in form, colouring and way of life, but they have certain common characteristics which justify their classification into a single family. They are essentially aquatic, three of their four toes being linked together by webs and the blunt, spatulate bill has a nail-like tip with a row of lamellae along the edge. These, with the use of the tongue, form a food-sifting apparatus rather like that of the flamingo. Being swimmers, it is necessary for them to waterproof their plumage efficiently and for this reason the preen gland is particularly large. In East Africa the family is represented by four species of geese and twenty of duck, ten of the latter being migrants from their breeding grounds in Europe and Asia during the non-breeding season.

Members of the family generally pass through a flightless period of some weeks after the breeding season which makes them especially vulnerable to predation. All the flight feathers moult simultaneously, unlike other birds, which shed them one after the other and so can continue to fly. The female, before the start of breeding, develops along its underparts specially long nest down feathers amongst the normal down, which she plucks out to line the nest cavity when the clutch of eggs is nearly complete. The two sexes differ in colour in a number of species, the female, which normally incubates, being less conspicuous all the year round. This enables it, during the time it is sitting, to blend with its environment and thus remain almost invisible. The male develops its nuptial plumage before pair formation and, in some cases, the colour of the beak also changes or intensifies.

The barge-like shape of most of the Anatidae is an adaptation for efficient swimming, helping the bird to keep its balance in rough conditions. The short legs are set wide apart on the broad frame and this causes the characteristic waddle on land, as the body is moved from side to side to maintain its centre of gravity.

In flight, the wings show a conspicuous patch of colour, sometimes white, but generally with a metallic sheen, and this is designed as a signal to help maintain cohesion in the flock. Ducks and geese are unable to glide to any extent, but some of them fly fast and with great endurance and wild geese have been recorded as high as 33,000 feet above sea-level. The vocal sounds uttered by the Anatidae are very numerous and these, combined with the typical movements associated with them, play a significant part in their lives, particularly during courtship and mating. A great deal of research has been carried out in this field by Konrad Lorenz and his co-workers. Some species dive for their food, which consists of vegetable and animal matter, whereas others are surface-feeders; geese feed by grazing, often some distance from water.

Below A pair of Spur-winged Geese. As these birds lose their flight feathers annually, they stay close to water, so they can swim away from predators.

Plate 23 Fulvous Tree Ducks *Dendrocygna bicolor*. Also known as whistling ducks, these are closely related to swans and geese.

Top to bottom The first
tentative steps of engaging
young Egyptian Geese as they
follow their mother.
Right, top and bottom
Mutual preening by a pair of
White-faced Tree Ducks.

Plate 24 Egyptian Geese *Alopochen aegyptiaca* were depicted on murals in the tombs of the ancient Egyptians.

Their nesting sites show considerable variety, most species nesting on the ground in thick vegetation, generally near water, while others prefer to nest on trees or in holes in trees, rocks or earth. Nesting is not usually colonial though there may be a great accumulation of nests at suitable sites. Simple hollow nests, initially lined with nearby vegetation and later by nest down are constructed. The number of eggs laid varies considerably, one egg being laid per day until the clutch is complete and incubation, generally carried out only by the female, begins with the last laid egg. The precocial young are covered with fine down when hatched and within a matter of hours, after the last egg has been hatched, the nestlings head for water with their mother. Ducklings feed independently from the first day and the parents' main function is to protect them, the female staying with the offspring until they are able to fly.

White-faced Tree Duck *Dendrocygna viduata*
Fulvous Tree Duck *Dendrocygna bicolor*
Also known as whistling ducks or whistling teals, these stand more erect than other ducks and show no difference between the sexes. They indulge in mutual preening and both the female and the male incubate eggs. The Fulvous has a remarkably wide range, occuring in North and South America, Africa and India.

The White-faced Tree Duck is about 18 inches long and readily distinguished by its white face and barred flanks. The Fulvous is slightly larger, and tawny rufus in colour with cream stripes along its flanks. Both species have a characteristic whistling call.

Right, bottom to top An Egyptian Goose takes off in rapid flight.
Above White-faced and Fulvous Tree Ducks are often found together.

Plate 25 A characteristic of the Spur-winged Geese *Plectropterus gambensis* is the little spur on the angle of their wings.

Plate 26 A Knob-billed Goose *Sarkidiornis melanotos* stands in splendid isolation, surrounded by water-lilies.

They frequent inland lakes and marshes in large flocks but their presence is irregular in that they may become absent for years and then reappear suddenly in abundance.

Egyptian Goose *Alopochen aegyptiaca*
Although well able to swim and dive, this species is often seen quite a distance away from water grazing on open plains, especially after the rains. It is 24 inches in size and has predominantly brown plumage with white shoulders and a chestnut spot on the breast. The call is a loud, strident honking and they nest in holes in trees, on rock ledges or on the ground in vegetation. The Egyptians regarded these birds as sacred and kept them in captivity. They are common in East Africa, being found in pairs or flocks on and around the fresh water lakes of the Rift Valley and elsewhere.

Spur-winged Goose *Plectropterus gambensis*
This is a large, powerful bird of almost 36 inches with a darkish red bill, and black upper parts which show a metallic gloss. The female is smaller than the male. During its annual moult it may be grounded for up to seven weeks and therefore prefers to stay near water during this period so that it can swim out when in danger. Unlike other ducks and geese, it has little specialized display and is silent, only occasionally uttering a high-pitched whistle.

Knob-billed Goose *Sarkidiornis melanotos*
Another nearly silent goose, it is readily distinguished by its black and white plumage, the black upper parts showing a greenish metallic sheen. The male (24 inches) is somewhat larger than the female and has a knob at the base of the bill.

Below A family of White-faced Tree Ducks. These ducks have a typical, whistling call.
Bottom White-faced and Fulvous Tree Ducks congregating at Lake Jipe, with the imposing North Para Mountains in the background.

10 Vultures

Old World vultures of the family Accipitridae bear a superficial resemblance in appearance and habits to the New World vultures, but are unrelated. In East Africa, vultures are represented by seven species, characterized by their predominantly carrion-feeding habits. However, the Egyptian Vulture *Neophron percnopterus* and Hooded Vultures *Neophron monachus* have been known to eat termites, the White-headed Vulture *Trigonoceps occipitalis* will kill game, and they will all eat insects such as locusts.

The head and neck are bare of feathers except for a thin covering of down, an adaptation for their practice of feeding on the viscera, and the hooked, powerful beak is designed to tear into the carcass. Most species have a distinct ruff of feathers at the base of the neck. The Palm-nut Vulture *Gypohierax angolensis* is an exception in that it is almost exclusively vegetarian and feeds mainly on the pulp which surrounds the kernel of the fruits of the Oil Palm and the Raffia Palm, as well as offal and dead fish.

Vultures are large eagle-like birds, 3½ to 15½ pounds in weight, having a wing span of 5 to 9 feet, and are capable of soaring for long periods. Their weak feet are not suitable for clutching prey, but are well adapted for walking and running. In East Africa they are found in all types of country and at all altitudes, but they are more characteristic of open plains and cultivated areas where large mammals are abundant.

Vultures fly high in search of food, often with other members of the same and related species, remaining aloft all day circling slowly and gliding in the rising thermals. Using

Below Ruppell's Griffon Vultures assemble in large numbers around a dead zebra.

Right, Plate 27   White-backed and
Ruppell's Griffon Vultures *Gyps africanus*
and *Gyps ruppellii*.
Below   The strong, hooked bill of a
Ruppell's Griffon Vulture enables it to tear
into a carcass.
Below centre   The Hooded Vulture
Neophron monachus has a thin slender bill.
Bottom   The Egyptian Vulture *Neophron
percnopterus* has discovered how to use rocks
as a means of breaking into ostrich eggs.

their keen eyesight, they observe the ground with its herds of animals and the movement of hyenas and jackals, and also the other lower flying carrion birds such as kites and ravens. When a vulture spies a corpse it planes down swiftly and is soon joined by others until numbers exceeding a hundred may be present. It is difficult for them to break into a large fresh carcass, unless they can make an entry through a wound, but a part-eaten carcass presents no problems. They probably never attack dying animals, but patiently wait nearby until all life is gone. The distended crop and gizzard can hold large amounts of meat, a quantity of nearly 13½ pounds having been found in the crop of a Griffon Vulture *Gyps fulvus*. They gorge heavily and feed to repletion if allowed to do so, as the meal may well have to last them for many days since feeding opportunities do not necessarily occur daily. The engorged birds find flying very difficult and may have to retire to the outskirts of the feeding group to stand and digest their meal.

On the Serengeti Plains in Tanzania in 1957, Jane and Hugo van Lawick-Goodall discovered the Egyptian Vulture's ability to use tools. When this vulture had failed to break open with its beak an ostrich's egg from an abandoned nest, it went in search of stones. The bird then returned with a stone in its beak, raised itself up and threw the stone down on the egg. At least four to five blows were required to crack this thick, hard shell.

African White-backed Vulture *Gyps africanus*
This is a common bird in East Africa. It is a large (32 inches) fulvous brown vulture with a distinct white back and rump, which distinguishes it from Ruppell's Griffon Vulture.

It prefers to live in open grasslands where trees occur along water courses and is rarely found in forests. It has a gregarious way of life, roosting, feeding and resting in company and its nest of sticks built on a tree, is strong enough to be used year after year. A single egg, which is incubated mostly by the female, hatches after about forty-five days and the chick develops very slowly, the fledgling leaving the nest at about 120 days.

Ruppell's Griffon Vulture *Gyps rueppellii*
Another gregarious bird, this vulture frequents both plains and mountains, avoiding human habitations. It is somewhat larger than the White-backed Vulture (34 inches), blackish-brown, with pale creamy tips to the feathers of the underparts and wing coverts, giving it a spotted appearance. It nests in colonies in cliffs and gorges, laying a single egg.

Below The Lappet-faced Vulture *Aegypius tracheliotus* is very large (40 inches), bare-headed with a massive bill.
Bottom This vulture shows its huge wing-span as it stretches out its wings to keep other vultures away from the prey.

II *Chanting Goshawks*

The genus *Melierax*, made up of three species, is widespread in Africa and not found elsewhere. The Dark Chanting Goshawk *M. metabates* and the Pale Chanting Goshawk *M. poliopterus* are medium-sized and harrier-like, whereas the Gabar Goshawk *M. gabar* is much smaller and more like a sparrow hawk in its habits. This genus has not been studied to any extent, so that further observations may indicate that these species are wrongly placed in their present order. The chanting goshawks have acquired their name because of their rather melodious call repeated for hours on end during the early breeding season.

Pale Chanting Goshawk *Melierax poliopterus*
This is a very upright-standing, pale grey hawk 19 inches long with bright reddish-orange legs, finely barred belly and a white rump which is conspicuous in flight. Although the Dark Chanting Goshawk is said to be darker grey, this is very difficult to differentiate in the field and the only reliable distinction in the plumage is the presence of dark bars on the rump in the case of the latter.

It is a resident of dry bush, semi-desert and acacia country. Found singly or in pairs, it has a fairly restricted home range and is usually found in and about the same group of trees. It can generally be observed perched on a tree, a telegraph pole, a rock or an ant-hill from which vantage point it makes brief hunting sorties. Unlike other hawks it spends considerable time on the ground walking about with ease and even running fast if necessary to pursue prey. Little time is spent flying any distance. Its main diet consists of lizards but it will also eat frogs, small snakes, grasshoppers and other insects and occasionally will even take small mammals.

When the breeding season starts, the male perches on a tall tree, chanting his display call for long hours. The call is also made on the wing and the pair can be seen to display soaring together in circles about 200 to 300 feet above the ground. Thorny acacias and euphorbias

Plate 28 The male Pale Chanting Goshawk *Melierax poliopterus* will perch and chant for hours during the breeding season.

are a favourite nesting site and a small flat nest with a shallow cup is built of sticks, lined with feathers, mud, rags and dung, about 10 to 30 feet above ground. It is used year after year and, when necessary, replaced by a new one nearby. One and sometimes two pale bluish- or greenish-white eggs are laid, in the latter case at several days' interval. It is believed that only the female incubates, and the eggs hatch also at different times. As a result only the first-hatched, stronger chick is reared. Much remains to be learnt about the incubation and the fledging periods of these species.

The Dark Chanting Goshawk perches on top of a tall, dead tree, scanning the surrounding area for suitable prey.

12 Fish Eagles

A group of buzzard-like birds closely related to the kites, the eight species of fish eagles and sea eagles make up the genus *Haliaeetus*. It is a cosmopolitan group, being absent only from South America, and consists of large birds of prey living mainly on fish. They include the White-tailed Sea Eagle *H. albicilla*, the American Bald Eagle *H. leucocephalus* and the African Fish Eagle *H. vocifer* of tropical Africa. They are characteristic birds of the seashore and large inland lakes, swamps and rivers.

Although fish form an important part of their food, this diet is by no means exclusive. The White-tailed Sea Eagle, which has been practically exterminated in Western Europe and is confined in a discontinuous distribution over a widespread range in northern parts of the Old World, relies for more than fifty per cent of its diet on a variety of water-birds such as coots, ducks and even swans, and small mammals the size of young roe deer, seal calves, rabbits and hares. It will also eat carrion and only a quarter of its food intake may be fish.

African Fish Eagle *Haliaeetus vocifer*

With the exception of the Madagascar Fish Eagle *H. vociferoides*, this eagle is the smallest of its genus, which includes some of the largest raptors, measuring about 30 inches. With its striking plumage of white head, chest, back and tail; chestnut wing coverts and belly; and black wings, it is readily identified as it sits prominently on a tall tree near water using the favourable viewpoint to spy for fish.

Another conspicuous feature is its characteristic call, so typical of Africa, which is made with the head thrown back and upwards, either on a perch or on the wing. The resultant sound is reminiscent of the laugh of one of the big gulls, but more piercing. Few of its daytime hours are spent on the wing, though at times it soars to considerable heights. During most of the day the eagle sits on its perch, often with its mate nearby, and even outside the breeding season there is a strong pair attachment, the couple being seldom apart. They usually roost together, often share the kill made by either of them and also keep in close touch by their call, the mate immediately replying to its partner. This often starts an outburst from other fish eagles if they are nearby and the resultant chorus of sound forever echoes in the ears of the listener.

Although it will feed on the young and adults of water-birds including ibises, storks, herons and particularly the Lesser Flamingo, and may even eat carrion at times, nine-tenths

Majestic African Fish Eagles are frequently seen perched with their mates as they have a strong pair-attachment even during the non-breeding season.

of its diet consists of fish. Most frequently this is caught by making short sorties from its vantage point on a tree, to which it returns if not successful. On a well-stocked lake its hunting range may not cover a square mile, whereas on a small river, a pair may require a ten-mile stretch to feed adequately. Small fish are snatched up by one foot from near the surface of water, but fish weighing 3 to 4 pounds require a special technique. In this case the bird makes a controlled descent, plunging down suddenly towards the end, digging its sharp claws into the prey, the pointed spines on the underside of its toes helping to grip the struggling fish. The prey is dragged along the surface of the water until at the last minute it is pulled up on a perch, though a very heavy catch is often eaten on the ground. Fish eagles frequently pursue Ospreys and other birds to pirate their catch, with varying success. They also regularly rob each other.

At breeding times the birds in their territories display by soaring, either singly or in pairs, calling loudly. A rare spectacular display takes place when the pair in flight grapple with each other with wings outstretched and legs extended, to come whirling down for hundreds of feet only to break away just before reaching the ground. Nests are built on large, tall trees and made of strong sticks lined with papyrus heads, grass, and often nests of weaver birds obtained from nearby colonies. In the first year, the nests may be four to five feet across and a foot thick, though in subsequent years, by further additions, it may become massive, reaching nearly six feet wide and four feet thick. If a pair is left undisturbed, it may build three nests, but they are not used in any particular sequence.

One to three, but usually two, white eggs are laid at three-day intervals. Incubation, usually by the female, starts on the first day with the result that the first hatched eaglet has a marked advantage over the others. Generally only one chick survives from a clutch of two, but two manage to live if three eggs have been laid. The incubation is for forty-five days and the fledgling takes its first flight at sixty-five to seventy-five days. The young require very close brooding at first and the female hardly ever leaves the nest, relying on the male to feed them. Only after about forty days does the female help to bring in food for the young. After the first flight the eaglet returns to roost at the nest for the next two weeks or so and then remains in the vicinity of the nest for a further two to three months. The life span of the African Fish Eagle is between twelve to sixteen years.

Plate 29   At breeding times, the magnificent African Fish Eagle *Haliaeetus vocifer* will display by soaring and calling loudly.

13 Kites

Generally speaking the term 'bird-of-prey' refers to a species that hunts and kills other animals for food; but more specifically, it is used to describe a member of the order Falconiformes. The word raptor is sometimes used interchangeably with bird-of-prey.

The largest family in this order is the Accipitridae and, in East Africa, it consists of eleven sub-families (including the Old World vultures) comprising some sixty-two species, which range from the tiny 9 to 11 inches of the Little Sparrow Hawk *Accipiter minullus* to the large and powerful 32 to 36 inches of the Crowned Hawk Eagle *Stephanoaetus coronatus*. In almost all these birds the female is larger than the male, sometimes appreciably so.

The characteristic pointed, down-curved bill and strong claws attached to powerful feet equip these species admirably to hunt and catch live prey, which forms their main diet. A few exceptions include the Old World vultures, and are carrion eaters. Most birds of prey are diurnal. They breed in trees although some also nest on crags. The nests are built of sticks and generally lined with grass and other green vegetation.

Three sub-families of the Accipitridae have already been discussed previously. Of these, the fish eagles of the genus *Haliaeetus* described in the preceding chapter belong to the sub-family Milvinae which, in East Africa, is represented by two genera, the other genus being *Milvus*, the true kites.

The many races of the Black Kite *Milvus migrans* species are widely dispersed throughout the Old World and Australia and may be regarded as one of the most common birds-of-prey, frequently seen around towns and villages, where they act as highly efficient scavengers and serve a very useful purpose. In parts of Asia and Africa they live inside towns, breeding in trees in the streets. Their diet, however, does not consist exclusively of carrion. They will take dead or stranded fish near water and will kill rabbits, mice, rats and other small mammals; also snakes, lizards and large insects.

White-tailed kites, as distinct from true kites, are members of the sub-family Elaninae and, in East Africa, its members consist of two species, the Black-shouldered Kite *Elanus caeruleus* and the smaller, most attractive Swallow-tailed Kite *Elanus riocourii*, which is a rare resident species, found only in Uganda and the northern parts of Kenya.

Black-shouldered Kite *Elanus caeruleus*

This thick-set hawk, about 13 inches long, pale blue-grey above and white below, has black 'shoulders' and a short, white, square tail. The eyes are strikingly red and all these unusual features combine to make it a very beautiful bird-of-prey. Both sexes are alike.

It has a slow graceful flight and could be readily mistaken for a seagull at a distance were it not for its very different habitat. It hovers like a kestrel, but with slow wing-beats. The bird's infrequent call is a clear piping whistle. Its habits and appearance are unlike other kites; perhaps, with the Swallow-tailed Kite, it has been wrongly classified.

It is sometimes said to use old nests of other birds, but its own nest, is a loose cup-shaped structure, lined with grass. Three to four eggs are laid and incubation is shared by both parents, the male often feeding the female, while she is sitting. The food consists of large insects and small animals such as birds, lizards, mice and rats.

It is a common species throughout Africa, where it frequents savanna and open country, farmland, mountain moorlands and margins of lakes and rivers. A plentiful supply of insects and rodents in an area may attract this bird in abundance.

A familiar sight near human habitations, the Black Kite is a highly efficient scavenger.

Plate 30 The Black-shouldered Kite *Elanus caeruleus* is a beautiful grey, black and white bird, often seen hovering, searching for prey.

14 Game Birds

Although the term 'game birds' is used ornithologically to refer to members of the order Galliformes, it is much more loosely used nowadays in various parts of the world to describe birds which are caught or killed for eating. In East Africa the order is represented by two families: Phasianidae with twenty-two species which include the quails, francolins, spurfowls and their allies, and Numididae, made up of four species of guinea-fowls. All are residents, with the exception of the Common Quail *Coturnix coturnix* which is a Palaearctic migrant. They are chicken-like birds and the sexes are usually alike. Their main food consists of seeds, insects, molluscs, roots and bulbs obtained by scratching with their feet.

Game birds are subject to game laws in a number of countries, by virtue of which they can only be shot with a licence. Whereas in most countries the laws are designed to protect them from excessive human predation, in the United Kingdom, curiously enough, the main purpose of their enaction seems to have been the protection of the sporting rights of the owner or occupier of the land on which they are found. In Kenya, all birds are totally protected with the exception of queleas and mouse-birds, regarded as agricultural pests, and game birds, which for the purposes of the Act include geese and ducks, francolins, partridges, quails, guinea-fowls, spurfowls, lesser bustards, snipe, sandgrouse, pigeons and doves. The capture and killing of the latter is stringently controlled by issue of limited licences during specified times of the year.

Yellow-necked Spurfowl *Francolinus leucoscepus*
Locally plentiful in East Africa, this is the most common francolin in Kenya and northern Tanzania, where it frequents edges of forest and woodland, and open bush and thornbush country. It is about the size of a domestic fowl, very upright in its stance even when running and is about 14 inches long. It has olive-brown upper parts with cream striations and

Plate 31 Helmeted Guineafowl *Numida meleagris*. These photogenic birds, with their distinctive spotted plumage, gather in large and noisy flocks.

buff-streaked dark brown underparts. Unlike other francolins, it has a conspicuous yellow throat becoming orange-red at its base and this characteristic makes it readily identifiable in the field. Both sexes are alike, except that the male has spurs on its legs.

A repeated loud, grating cry uttered particularly in the early morning and late afternoon, is typical of this bird. It occurs in small parties and when disturbed, prefers to run away, only taking to its wings as a last resort. Its nest is a mere scrape in the ground, generally near a tuft of grass or under a bush, lined with grass. Three to eight eggs are laid, and hatch in eighteen to twenty days. The young leave the nest within twenty-four hours of hatching.

Helmeted Guinea-fowl *Numida meleagris*

This is a locally abundant and attractive game bird with its general black colour thickly spotted all over with white. A bony crest or horn protrudes from the crown of its head, which together with the neck is thinly feathered. A large bird (22 inches), it is usually seen in pairs or large flocks. But these flocks are not as large as they used to be in the past, when some numbered as many as 2000. It has been killed extensively for the pot, its last stronghold perhaps being the Masai areas in Kenya and Tanzania where it is numerous.

The birds in their large flocks roost on nearby trees and awake early at first light. After a vociferous dawn chorus of a loud cackling call often repeated, they descend to the ground and make their leisurely way to water eating as they go, their food consisting of insects, seeds and roots. More foraging for food takes place after the morning drink and dust bath, but during the hot time of the day the birds make their way into shady shelters leaving only a sentinel to keep watch and sound the alarm. Apart from humans, there is very little evidence of other predators, an example of the success of their extreme wariness; however, when they make their way back to their roost in the evening, they greet the setting sun with another loud chorus, which attracts the hunter with his gun.

Little is known of their courting habits, if any, but during the breeding season the birds pair off and become silent and secretive. Up to twenty eggs may be laid in a hollow in the ground, generally well hidden in a thicket.

Below The Crested Francolin *Francolinus sephaena* is a game bird found in semi-desert country.
Bottom, Plate 32 A male Yellow-necked Spurfowl *Francolinus leucoscepus*. The spurs on its legs can be seen in this picture.

15 Cranes

The fourteen to fifteen species of the crane family Gruidae are large, stately, long-necked and long-legged birds with a superficial resemblance to storks, to which they are however in no way related. Their calls have been variously described as trumpet-like, honking and goose-like, but they have one feature in common: the loudness and penetrating power, which is due to the remarkable development of the windpipe. They inhabit open country, marshlands and cultivated areas where their diet consists of vegetable matter, grain, large insects, mice and small reptiles.

All the northern species are migratory. Although not gregarious during the breeding season, some species gather together in large flocks afterwards and fly in a straight or V-formation, with their necks extended forwards, unlike the herons. The deliberate, slow beat of the wings give the false impression that they are not strong fliers. It is during flight that their resounding call is most often heard. Inevitably their numbers are affected by human predation, but even more, the systematic drainage and clearing of swampy areas in which they prefer to breed brings about serious reductions. The Common Crane *Grus grus* is now thus extinct as a breeding species in many European countries, although the catholicity of its diet helps to sustain it in some places.

The Whooping Crane *Grus americana* is a prime example of a species endangered by the lack of suitable quarters in winter, during which this bird continues to be territorial. It is only found in North America and Canada in very limited numbers, the local world population being as small as twenty in 1940. Even twenty-five years later their numbers had only increased to fifty in their wild state although a few more had been bred in captivity. Despite strenuous conservation measures there is a serious danger of the Whooping Crane becoming extinct.

To conserve this rare bird, it was suggested that some cranes should be caught when in total moult and therefore flightless, and bred in captivity. Despite vigorous opposition from certain conservation organizations, one bird was captured in this way, but soon died as a result of heat exhaustion brought about by its treatment. It was then decided to try another method, one which had been used with some success with other endangered species. From a normal clutch of two eggs, the Whooping Crane usually rears only one young. Therefore single eggs were collected from some nests and hatched artificially. The birds so obtained formed the nucleus of a breeding stock in captivity. But the important question remains: where will these new additions find suitable winter quarters?

The family Gruidae is represented in East Africa by three species.

Crowned Crane *Balearica regulorum*

With its black velvety crown, distinctive 'fan' of straw-coloured bristle-like feathers on the nape, bare cheeks, red and white neck wattles, black primaries and chestnut secondaries, this crane may well be described as one of the most beautiful of the larger African birds. It is about 40 inches long and the sexes are alike.

It is widely distributed in Africa and abundant in Uganda, where it is the national emblem of the country. Outside the breeding season this crane is highly gregarious and is found in large flocks in their hundreds, though groups of fifteen to sixteen are more common. Its loud, melodious, plaintive cry made up of two syllables, heard usually when the bird is in flight, is unforgettable. Locusts and other insects, vegetation, grain, frogs and small reptiles form its diet. It walks about stamping its feet on the ground to disturb its prey, on open plains, marshes, swamps and cultivated land.

A pair of cranes or even more perform a ceremonial dance which is fascinating to watch. There is some doubt whether it is strictly a courtship ritual as it seems to be performed at all times of the year and sometimes by juveniles. The birds open their wings wide, stiffly bow to each other and then suddenly leap two or three feet up in the air, coming down to run around each other and start the process all over again. It is likely that the birds pair for life. A space is trampled down in a swamp and lined with rushes, reeds etc., to form a nest in which two or three eggs are laid and the couple, having left the flock, become solitary. The downy young, which run about soon after hatching, are cared for by both parents.

Right The striking straw-coloured 'fan', black velvety crown and red wattle make the Crowned Crane a very attractive bird.
Overleaf, Plate 33 With its fine head-dress, the Crowned Crane *Balearica pavonina* is among the most decorative of African birds.

16 Plovers

Consisting as it does of about eleven genera divided into some sixty-two species, this family (Charadriidae) is distributed throughout the main zoogeographic regions, particularly in the tropics. Some species make remarkably long journeys on migration to their breeding areas situated at higher altitudes. Plovers of the genus *Vanellus* are known as lapwings, sometimes classified as a separate sub-family.

Plovers are small- to medium-sized birds, with a thickset head and neck on a compact body. Their plumage, of a marked colour pattern, makes them easy to see, but it is surprising how easily they can merge into the background when necessary. This is particularly so of the chicks, whose markings provide excellent camouflage. The young crouch down on a warning call from the parents, which then proceed to divert the attention of the intruder by spreading wide one of their wings and acting as if injured, a form of distraction display quite common among plovers. They are often seen on bare ground, near water on the coast and inland lakes, short grasslands or similar open situations. Plovers are strong fliers and can run swiftly. Their food consists of insects, molluscs, worms and some vegetation. When catching prey, the bird will make a short, smart dash towards it, stop suddenly and then make a final scurry to grab it.

The nest is built on the ground and consists of a shallow indentation, quite often unlined, in which are laid two to five eggs with dark markings on a pale buff or grey background, an effective camouflage. Both parents incubate and look after the young, which are ready to leave the nest immediately their down feathers are dry.

Blacksmith Plover *Vanellus armatus*
Perhaps the best known of all in East Africa, this plover has distinctive black, white and grey plumage. It is about 11 inches long and is found from the southern half of Kenya, to South Africa. It has a white crown and black and grey back. It is most common in the vicinity of fresh or brackish water, near lakes, rivers, mudflats and swamps where it finds its main diet of insects, worms and crustacea.

Below A Crowned Plover crouches over its chick to shade it from the harsh sun.
Bottom, Plate 34 Crowned Plover *Vanellus coronatus*. The black-and-white markings on its head resemble a schoolboy's cap.
Overleaf, Plate 35 Blacksmith Plover *Vanellus armatus*. This bird gets its name from the loud cry, like a hammer hitting an anvil, that it makes when disturbed.

Above A Kittlitz's Sand Plover at its nest. It has covered its eggs with sand to protect them from predators.

Plate 36 The Three-banded Plover *Charadrius tricollaris* is distinctively marked, with its red eye and orange and black-tipped bill.

Overleaf, Plate 37 Spurwing Plovers *Vanellus spinosus* make an attractive pattern against a backdrop of gently breaking waves.

The nest is a shallow depression and may even be the hoof print of a large mammal, usually lined with grass and is generally built near water but not necessarily on its edge. Sometimes the two eggs are laid in dried droppings of elephants or buffaloes. This plover is normally silent but becomes very aggressive and noisy during breeding time. The bird flies repeatedly and fearlessly at the enemy, making dive-bombing attacks and uttering its characteristic metallic cry suggestive of a hammer hitting an anvil, the sound from which it derives its name.

Spurwing Plover *Vanellus spinosus*

This is only marginally smaller than the Blacksmith Plover, from which it is easily distinguished by its light greyish-brown back and black crown. The wings and tail are black and white, the pattern being particularly conspicuous in flight. The small spur on its wing is not readily seen in the field. Although predominantly a resident species in Africa, in recent years, it has been found to breed in Greece.

Normally seen singly or in pairs, occasionally they are present in small flocks, especially after breeding. Found in the vicinity of water, especially near areas of short grass, this plover occurs alongside the Blacksmith Plover in some places. It is also normally silent, but vociferous, aggressive and fearless if disturbed at the nest or when young are present.

Crowned Plover *Vanellus coronatus*

Unlike the two species mentioned above, this plover inhabits short grassy plains and open bush country where it may be found in loose-knit groups of twenty or so. It is local and commonly resident throughout East and Central Africa at all altitudes.

With its white abdomen, pale greyish upper parts, red legs, red bill with a black tip, and the black head with a white ring on the crown (curiously reminiscent of a schoolboy cap) the Crowned Plover is a handsome bird. The bird, when alarmed, will make a quiet scolding sound to begin with, but if the intrusion continues, this will rise to a high-pitched shriek as it carries out dive-bombing attacks.

Kittlitz's Sand Plover *Charadrius pecuarius*

This small plover (6 inches) has dark upperparts, pale underparts with an orangy-buff wash and a white band on its forehead which continues round the back of the neck to form a white collar. In suitable localities, which are sandy or consist of mudflats on the coast and inland waters, Kittlitz's Sand Plover is found in small or sometimes large flocks up to a hundred, especially during the non-breeding season.

The nest is an indentation in the sand, not necessarily close to water, and the eggs are usually covered over. It is said that the female, as she leaves the nest, kicks sand over the eggs to hide them. Incubation may well take the form of shading the sand-covered area. This plover has a plaintive cry and will carry out the injured-wing distraction display when its young are subjected to predation by raptors.

Three-banded Plover *Charadrius tricollaris*

Another smallish plover (7 inches), it is widespread throughout East and Central Africa, on shores of lakes, streams, rivers, dams and pools, but is rare at the coast. It is readily recognized by the presence of two black bands separated by a white band across the breast. Its upper parts are darkish olive-brown. The red eye, orange bill with a black tip and the white ring on the crown makes this a distinctive species. Usually found in pairs, it is not as numerous as Kittlitz's Sand Plover. The nest is a scrape in the ground in which two eggs are normally laid. They are not covered with sand but their markings provide a good camouflage. It also has a plaintive cry when disturbed.

Below left With a flurry of feathers, a Spurwing Plover reacts aggressively when a Glossy Ibis intrudes on its territory.

Below The Three-banded Plover is well-camouflaged at its nest among the rocks.
Below centre The plover's eggs, laid in a slight, unlined hollow merge with their background and are hard to find.
Bottom The boldly-patterned Spurwing Plover is easily identified by its black, white and greyish-brown plumage.

17 Snipe and Sandpipers

About eighty species make up the family Scolopacidae, but a general term 'snipe and sandpipers' is reasonably acceptable since sandpipers form the majority of the family. In East Africa it is represented by thirty species, all of them Palaearctic migrants with the exception of the African Snipe *Gallinago nigripennis*, which is a resident. The family consists of a group of small- to medium-sized waders with long legs, long pointed wings and a slender bill which may be either straight, up-curved or down-curved. The sexes are generally alike, but in many species the winter plumage is paler and markedly different from the summer breeding dress which sometimes has black and reddish-brown on the underparts.

The East Africa visitors are migrants from Europe and Asia during the non-breeding season, their chief breeding areas being the arctic or sub-arctic regions. Many species are highly gregarious in their winter quarters in Africa, though others are solitary. Some of them remain in Eastern Africa during the Palaearctic summer, but these are usually non-breeding birds, the majority of whom do not develop their full breeding plumage. Most of the members are highly migratory and widespread over the world when not breeding. Always associated with water, these birds obtain their food, consisting mainly of worms, insects and crustacea, by probing with their beaks in mud or sand, exposed or in shallow water. When resting they adopt the characteristic posture of standing on one leg with the head tucked into the feathers of the back.

Nests are almost invariably on the ground, sometimes concealed in grass, but generally completely in the open and the scrapes in which the eggs are laid are rarely lined with vegetation. This makes the eggs very vulnerable to predation and therefore they have evolved colours and patterns by virtue of which they are 'lost' against the background. Even those eggs obvious to the human eye may still be invisible to the predator which may not be able to distinguish different colours.

Apparently only two colour pigments, one blue and the other reddish-brown, are required to produce the remarkably wide range of colours and markings of birds' eggs. Depending on the absence or presence of these pigments, their concentration and shape, and whether they are laid down on the surface or at different depths of the partially transparent shell, any colour and pattern can be produced. A badly camouflaged and therefore conspicuous egg would be readily taken whereas the cryptic egg would survive and thus the evolution of the least vulnerable, successfully-patterned egg would continue.

Below and below centre A Curlew Sandpiper shows its characteristic roosting and preening postures.

Bottom, Plate 38 Curlew Sandpiper *Calidris ferruginea*. It is a long journey from the Curlew Sandpiper's breeding-ground in Siberia to its temporary home in Africa.

Right, Plate 39 The colours of the Little Stint *Calidris minuta* blend attractively with its surroundings.
Below Migrant waders collect in large numbers on the shores of Lake Turkana during the winter.
Bottom The graceful Greenshank forages for food along the shore of the lake.

Greenshank *Tringa nebularia*

This graceful long-legged bird is widespread and often a common winter visitor and passage migrant throughout the Ethiopian Region in suitable areas. It is about 12 inches long, pale sepia above and white below with a slightly up-curved bill. In its breeding plumage it has some dark markings on the upper parts.

It is common along the coast and on inland lakes during the spring migration and non-breeding birds often spend their summer in Africa. The widespread breeding ground extends from Scotland across Europe to Siberia. Its call is unmistakable, a loud two or three note 'chew-chew-chew'.

Curlew Sandpiper *Calidris ferruginea*

From its relatively localized breeding range in north-east Siberia, this sandpiper makes its way in a south-westerly direction in the summer and depending on the prevailing winds at the time, it may well span the world in its migration. Autumn passage migrants occur annually in Great Britain and appear in large numbers in some years.

The Curlew Sandpiper arrives in its winter dress of pale grey above and white below. With its slightly down-curved bill and the distinct white rump in flight, it is readily identified. The summer plumage, consisting mainly of chestnut-red, but still with a white rump, is acquired from mid-April onwards and since it lingers as late as the end of May, large numbers of them can be seen with other waders at Mida Creek on the Kenya coast during this time, all in their summer dress.

Little Stint *Calidris minuta*

The smallest (5 inches) of the winter visitors to East and Central Africa, some have already arrived by the beginning of August, having left their breeding area in Russia to make their migratory way across the eastern Mediterranean. By the end of September they are present in large numbers on the coastal mudflats and tidal sands, and on expanses of exposed mud near inland waters.

The most marked change from winter to summer dress is that the mottled grey upper parts and the whitish chest mainly become rufous.

Below A flock of mixed waders at Lake Turkana. These gregarious birds can be seen probing for worms and crustacea at the water's edge.
Bottom, Plate 40 Greenshank *Tringa nebularia*. This bird is a common winter visitor throughout the Ethiopian Region.

18 Avocets and Stilts

The family Recurvirostridae is quite small, consisting of four species of avocets, two species of stilts and the Ibis-bill, but has an almost worldwide distribution. In the Ethiopian Region it is represented by the Avocet and the Black-winged Stilt, both of which are resident in small numbers, augumented by large or very large numbers of Palaearctic migrants during the winter season.

Avocet *Recurvirostra avosetta*

This medium-sized bird (17 inches) is easily recognizable by its contrasting black and white plumage; long thin, black upturned bill and long greyish-blue legs. The legs extend well back beyond the tail in flight. The resident population is small and very local, generally found on the Rift Valley lakes, where it is an irregular breeder, with the exception of Lake Magadi where it breeds regularly between April and June in most years. But come the European winter, and the Palaearctic avocets travel in their hundreds and thousands, to range throughout Eastern Africa.

They frequent fresh and brackish water lakes, exposed mudflats, estuaries and sand banks, Lakes Naivasha, Elmenteita and Nakuru in Kenya being particularly popular in winter. With its up-curved bill slightly open, the Avocet walks through shallow water, sweeping its beak from side to side sifting out the food, consisting of aquatic insects, small molluscs and crustacea. Sometimes food is also found in deep water or muddy rivulets.

Avocets carry out a variety of displays during the breeding season: social, aggressive and sexual. Each territory is defended vigorously but the elaborate ceremonial display prior to mating merits special attention. The female invites the male by adopting a crouching posture with its outstretched neck held in such a way that its bill and head are practically touching the water. The male approaches preening constantly and walking from one side of her to the other until he brushes against her tail. He then mounts her and after mating jumps off. The pairs cross bills and run ashore along slightly divergent paths, which eventually separating when they reach the sand.

Below The purposeful stride of a Black-winged Stilt shows off its extraordinarily long legs.
Bottom, Plate 41 Easily recognizable by their contrasting plumage, Avocets *Recurvirostra avosetta* have a variety of ceremonial displays.

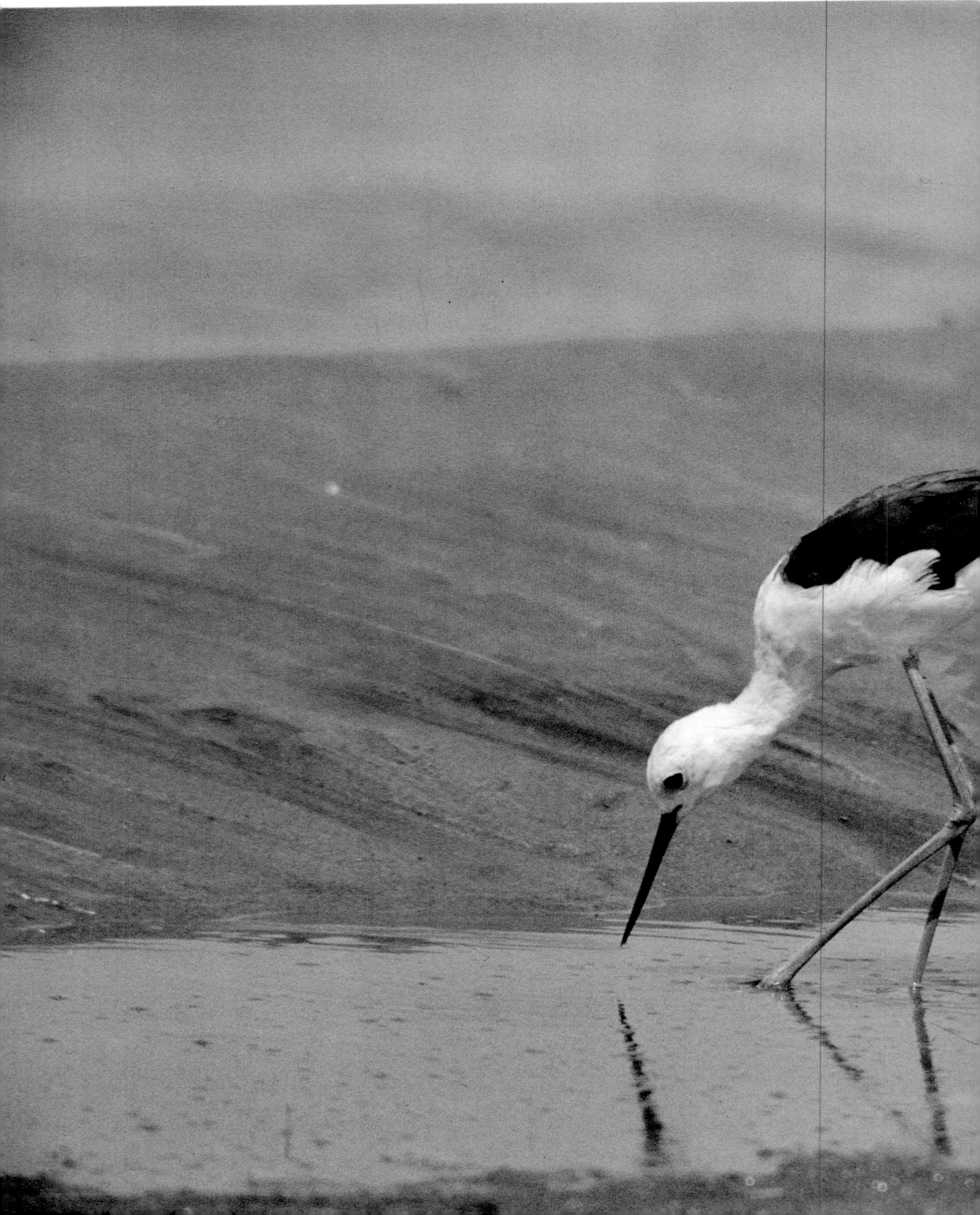

Above and top The Avocet at its nest on stony ground. During the day the bird will stand over the eggs to shade them from the sun.
Left, Plate 42 Balanced on spindly legs, the Black-winged Stilt *Himantopus himantopus* searches determinedly for food.

Nests, generally in colonies, are scrapes in dried mud or sand, lined with grass or stones only if suitable material is available nearby. The usual number of eggs is four, which are incubated by both parents, who take turns sitting on them, or shading them from the sun .

The eggs hatch at between twenty-two and twenty-four days and the young, which are ready to leave the nest within hours of hatching, move off with the parents to the nearest water where they are at once able to swim quite safely, and start to feed themselves forthwith using their short straight beaks for pecking. The adults continue to tend the young until they are independent of them in about ten weeks.

Black-winged Stilt *Himantopus himantopus*

Another species with a long, black, thin bill, but this time not curved, with plumage of black wings and back in sharp contrast to the white head, neck and underparts, this bird is unmistakable on the ground or in the air. With its extraordinary vermilion-red legs, longer in proportion to the body than all birds with the exception of the flamingo, the stilt is 15 inches long. The legs trail behind conspicuously in flight, form an odd-looking inverted V on either side of the body when it is sitting and force it to flex its legs considerably when feeding on the ground or in shallow water. It is however, well adapted for feeding in deeper water and its diet consists mainly of beetles, tadpoles, and aquatic insects and their larvae.

The Black-winged Stilt is an uncommon local resident in East Africa, where it breeds in a few isolated areas and is supplemented with a large influx of Palaearctic migrants during the winter months. It is an almost worldwide species and is found throughout Eastern Africa where it frequents fresh and brackish water areas inland but is uncommon at the coast. Usually seen singly or in pairs and rarely in small groups, it is partial to alkaline lakes.

Where suitable conditions exist, its nest is built up from the bottom with reeds, stalks and mud to float just above the surface of the water. In dry areas, however, it is a mere scrape in the ground, three or four eggs being laid which are incubated by both sexes. The downy young are ready to leave the nest soon after they are hatched at about twenty-five to twenty–six days. The parents are adept at the injured-wing diversion if disturbed.

Below The Avocet lays its eggs in a slight hollow on the pebbly ground.
Bottom Parent Avocets share the task of shading the eggs. Here one prepares to relieve its mate at the nest.

19 Stone Curlews

The family Burhinidae is represented in the Ethiopian Region by four species, one of which, the European Stone Curlew *Burhinus oedicnemus*, is a winter migrant to Uganda and Kenya from the Palaearctic Region. A number of different common names in various parts of the world and the term 'thicknee' is obviously based on the very marked thickening of the intertarsal joint commonly mistaken for the knee. In some respects thicknees resemble bustards, but in others, they are more like plovers. They are strange-looking birds, 14 to 20 inches long, with their large heads and big yellow eyes, the size of the latter being adapted for their mainly nocturnal habits. They eat a great variety of food including insects, worms and seeds.

Thicknees are habitually watchful and they spend the day standing or sitting motionless in the shade. Like all birds they are particularly vulnerable when at the nest or with young, but here they are helped by the fact that the colouring of both the adult and the young enables them to almost disappear into their surroundings, despite their prominent yellow eyes. When approached they will flatten themselves on the ground with heads and neck outstretched. The fact that thicknees are silent and unobtrusive during the daytime maybe another defence mechanism.

Plate 43 Water Dikkop *Burhinus vermiculatis*. This curious, nocturnal bird keeps very still during the day, blending with its surroundings.

When flushed, the sitting bird will leave the nest furtively in a crouching run with its neck retracted, flying with some reluctance and then only for a short distance. However, when it does fly, it does so low and silently and the speed of its movement can be quite deceptive. Although sometimes found in small parties, it is essentially a solitary bird and will resist mixing with other species.

Most of its activity is confined to the night, when it can become quite noisy, especially during the breeding season. The two eggs are laid in an unlined scrape in the ground, sometimes decorated with pebbles, and their markings harmonize well with the surroundings. Both sexes take it in turn to incubate, when they sit upright and motionless to avoid drawing attention to themselves. The incubation period is twenty-five to twenty-seven days and the young, being highly precocial, leave the nest actively on the day they are hatched.

Spotted Stone Curlew or **Spotted Thicknee** *Burhinus capensis*
This is widespread and local throughout East Africa, but not easy to see because of its colouring which camouflages the bird most effectively. The upper parts appear heavily spotted because of dense streaking on the tawny-buff background. The underparts are pale buff and with broad black streaks on the throat and chest. Both sexes are alike and the size is 17 inches. As in the case of owls and nightjars the large yellow eye is designed for effective nocturnal use. It frequents arid bush and lightly wooded country, dry rocky beds and other similar habitats. This bird is often seen on roads at night, and a number are killed by motor vehicles.

Water Dikkop *Burhinus vermiculatus*
This is somewhat smaller than the Spotted Thicknee and greyer, with dark striations on the back. It is also widespread but is found near water, on riverbanks and lake shores. Its eggs are sometimes laid in dried droppings of the larger mammals such as elephant and buffalo. For some unexplained reason the Water Dikkop has the curious habit of also making its nest amongst crocodiles, if they are present.

20 Coursers

The family Glareolidae is divided into two sub-families, the pratincoles and the coursers, the latter being a small group whose distribution is restricted to the warmer regions of the Old World. There are seven resident species of coursers in Africa, of which the Cream-coloured Courser *Cursorius cursor* is found in Kenya, Somalia and Ethiopia as well and the Egyptian Plover *Pluvianus aegyptius* is found only in Uganda. They are plover-like birds with elongated legs and pointed bills and, with the exception of the Egyptian Plover, predominantly light or dark brown. The sexes are alike. The coursers inhabit semi-desert, arid areas and can be seen in pairs or small family parties on bare ground or in very short grass. Their diet is entirely made up of insects, mainly beetles and grasshoppers.

No nests are built and eggs are laid directly on the ground, their colour and markings making for a perfect camouflage. The normal clutch is two or three, but the Two-banded Courser lays only one egg.

The Egyptian Plover differs considerably from other members of the sub-family. Besides being much more distinctively marked, it prefers to live on the sandbanks of rivers and has some strange nesting habits. The eggs are buried in the sand, the heat of which presumably provides the required temperature for incubation. The female broods the mound under which they are buried and this may be to shade the eggs and so prevent them from overheating. When in danger, the chicks are also buried and the adult has been observed to keep the sand above them moist and cool by spewing water over it, which it had previously swallowed.

A number of stories exist from the time of Herodotus, the Greek historian, to the effect that the Egyptian Plover flies into the mouth of the crocodile to pick out meat particles from between its teeth and leeches from its jaws, thus keeping the mouth clean. In return the crocodile does not harm the bird. This story has been repeated uncritically many times since, but no proof has been given of its authenticity. It is no doubt true that the Egyptian Plover runs fearlessly amongst crocodiles and sometimes even on their backs in its search for food, but no conscientious scientist has observed its entry into the reptile's mouth.

Two-banded Courser *Rhinoptilus africanus*

This small species (8 inches) is mottled buff and black above; and the underparts are buffish-white in colour with two conspicuous black bands on the chest. It is a local resident on open plains in Central Kenya and Tanzania but not common elsewhere.

No nest is built, the single egg being laid on the bare ground generally in full sun. This makes it necessary for the bird to crouch over the egg during daytime to shade it from the heat and both parents take turns to protect it.

Below The Pratincole *Glareola pratincola*, although closely related to the coursers, belongs to a different sub-family and, with its short legs, looks rather like a tern.
Bottom left, Plate 44 Spotted Stone Curlews *Burhinus capensis*. These birds are well-camouflaged, and if approached will flatten themselves on the ground.
Top left The nocturnal Spotted Stone Curlew is a strange-looking bird, with its large, specially adapted eyes.

Plate 45 Two-banded Courser *Rhinoptilus africanus*. This clearly shows the distinctively-patterned plumage.

21 Sandgrouse

The sixteen species which make up the family Pteroclididae reside mainly in Africa and Asia, but two of them are also found in parts of Europe in variable numbers. There is considerable controversy regarding the classification of the sandgrouse family, but it has closer affinity to the pigeons than to any other family, such as the grouse, and for this reason is classified next to the former. Sandgrouse are about the size of pigeons and are terrestrial birds which, with a few exceptions, inhabit semi-desert country. Their colouring resembles the area in which they live but the male, which is unlike the female, tends to be more brightly coloured. Their diet is entirely vegetarian, consisting mainly of seeds of various grasses and grain, and rarely berries and roots.

The nest is a depression in the ground, sometimes a natural one, enlarged by the bird turning its body in it to enlarge the hole. It may be near a bush or out in the open and is generally unlined. Three eggs are usually laid, and incubated by both sexes, the male taking the long night stretch. When hatched the young are covered with down and are ready to leave the nest as soon as they are dry. They can feed themselves but rely on the parents to supply their need for water. Their special way of doing this is described below.

Because of the hot, semi-arid areas in which they live and their diet of grain, the sandgrouse need to drink regularly, at least once a day and when the weather is very hot, sometimes twice. This may necessitate a flight of up to fifty miles to the source of water and this is made either at dawn or near sunset, each species having a specific time schedule of quite remarkable accuracy. Although sandgrouse are sometimes flushed in pairs or singly during daytime, they are naturally gregarious and will gather in flocks before flying to water, being joined by more on the way. Flying in a steady stream, they may number hundreds or even thousands. Their cruising speed is between forty and fifty miles per hour and therefore they are able to cover a distance of as much as fifty miles in about an hour. Their large numbers and the consequent noise inevitably make them vulnerable to predation and therefore, as soon as they reach their drinking place, they go straight down, drink their fill within twenty to thirty seconds and leave immediately.

The period of incubation makes it necessary for the birds to water in turn and once the young are hatched, the necessity of supplying them with water arises. This function is normally carried out by the male. After drinking its fill, the sandgrouse crouches down in the water and thoroughly soaks its belly feathers. It then slowly makes its rather long

Below, Plate 46 Chestnut-bellied Sandgrouse *Pterocles exustus.*
Below left The Abyssinian Nightjar *Caprimulgus policephalus* relies on camouflage to escape detection in the daytime.
Right The camouflage-patterned Sandgrouse eggs are laid in a hollow, scraped out near a bush.

journey back to the nest area where the young are being looked after by the female. The male stands upright with its feathers fluffed out, the chicks crouch under and draw the water out of the plumage with their beaks. This method was doubted for a long time but Cade and Maclean have been able to confirm it by their observations. They found that the belly feathers of the Namaqua Sandgrouse *Pterocles namaqua*, because of their highly specialized barbules, not only held three times as much water as the corresponding feathers of other birds, but maintained their structure in spite of the regular wetting and sucking. A normal feather would soon begin to fray as a result. A female can also carry water, though perhaps not so efficiently, if for some reason the male is not available to do so.

Chestnut-bellied Sandgrouse *Pterocles exustus*

This is a sandgrouse 12 inches long, in which the upper parts of the male are sandy-brown and in the female are streaked and barred buff and brown. Their central tail feathers are long and thin.

They gather in large flocks and fly to water, generally in the morning and may do so again in the afternoon if the weather is hot. This is the most common sandgrouse in most parts of Kenya and northern Tanzania where it inhabits arid bush country and plains.

22 Pigeons and Doves

The family Columbidae is quite a large one consisting of about 280 species which are widespread in temperate and tropical areas of the world and absent only from the polar regions. The term 'pigeon' is used for the larger species and 'doves' for the smaller ones but this is not an invariable rule. They occur in Africa at all altitudes and in all types of country, no part being without one or more resident species. They number twenty-one, of which five are found only in Uganda and one is confined to Kenya. Pigeons and doves are small- to medium-sized birds with small round heads, and have a plump, compact body, densely covered with soft plumage. The beak is fairly small with a hard tip, but is soft at the base. Although different members of the family utter a variety of calls, their most characteristic sound is a deep cooing or crooning call by which they are well known. The two sexes may be alike; the female a duller version of the male, or they may differ strikingly.

Out of the breeding season they tend to be gregarious and are often seen in large flocks. They are strong fliers, the Green Pigeon *Treron australis* perhaps being the fastest. Their main food consists of berries, seeds, and buds; and the way they drink by immersing their bills in the water and sucking, instead of putting their heads up to swallow, is very unusual in birds, and characteristic of this family.

Their nests give the impression of being flimsy, but the twigs and greenery woven into their construction make them quite strong. Two eggs are normally laid, incubated in turn by both parents, which also tend the young. These are covered with a yellowish down when born, and are quite helpless. The young bird inserts its bill deep into the parent's mouth and is fed by regurgitation from the crop. For the first few days its food consists exclusively of 'pigeon's milk', which is made up of the cells of the epithelium of the crop. The lining of the crop thickens and fatty layers are laid down during incubation, the cells proliferate, slough off and mix with the globules to form the milk. The diet is gradually augmented by seeds and fruit, and in about three to four weeks the young can fend for themselves.

The extinction of the North American Passenger Pigeon *Ectopistes migratorius* is a spectacular story of a species which numbered millions in the nineteenth century and became extinct by the beginning of the twentieth. The last bird in its wild state was killed in 1900 and the last survivor in captivity died in 1914. Although human predation is blamed for the extermination, there is considerable controversy as to whether this is so. There is little doubt that this species was particularly vulnerable because of its remarkably gregarious nature, as it nested and migrated in enormous numbers. But it is also believed by certain authorities that this pigeon was a relatively slow and inefficient breeder and did not replace itself in sufficient numbers to maintain an effective density of population, more birds dying than were born.

Speckled Pigeon *Columba guinea*
This is a large pigeon (16 inches) which inhabits open country, acacia woodlands and cultivated areas where it is seen feeding in small flocks, mostly on the ground. It is readily recognizable by its brownish back and wings, the latter with white spots and grey underparts. The sexes are alike and its call is a series of deep 'coos'.

Pink-breasted Dove *Streptopelia lugens*
A small bird (11 inches), its colour is dark grey with a dark patch on each side of the neck and a chestnut patch on each wing. It is a bird of high altitude forest areas and is common in the Aberdares, and somewhat less so around Nairobi.

Left The Red-eyed Dove *Streptopelia semitorquata* is very common and one of three species in this family characterized by a half-collar on the hind-neck.
Right, Plate 47 Pink-breasted Dove *Streptopelia lugens*.
Overleaf, Plate 48 Speckled Pigeons *Columba guinea*. Pigeons have an unusual method of drinking, sucking at the water rather than putting their heads back, like other birds.

23 Owls

Owls belong to the distinct order Strigiformes, whose members are found in different habitats all over the world including deserts. The group is divided into two families, the Tytonidae or barn owls consisting of ten species, all belonging to the genus *Tyto*; and the Strigidae, commonly distinguished as typical owls, which number over 120. Mention may be made of the Barn Owl *Tyto alba*, perhaps the most familiar of all, because of its nearly worldwide distribution. The two families differ only slightly in their skeletal structure and some taxonomists consider them to be a single family divided into two sub-families.

In Africa there are three members of the genus *Tyto* and seventeen species of the Strigidae, the latter showing considerable variation in their size, colouration and habits. Of these, two are Palaearctic migrants and two are endemic, one restricted to Tanzania and the other to Kenya. Mrs Morden's Scops Owl *Otus ireneae* is known to exist only in the Sokoke-Arabuko lowland coastal rain-forest north of Mombasa in Kenya, and serious concern is felt amongst naturalists about its survival, due to man's destruction of its habitat.

Owls are easily recognized by the big, round head set, apparently without a neck, on a short-tailed, soft-plumed body, and their most distinctive feature, a facial disc in which the two large eyes are directed forward. Some of them have 'ear' tufts set on either side of the head. Their sizes range from the 7 inches of the tiny Scops Owl *Otus scops* to the 20 to 26 inches of the large impressive eagle owls. The female is usually somewhat larger than the male but the difference is not so marked as in the diurnal birds-of-prey. Owls make a variety of calls including hooting, whistling, screeching, hissing and even barking.

This order shows a number of features which have evolved as a result of their predominantly nocturnal habits. Both male and female (with the exception of the Snowy Owl *Nyctea scandiaca*) are alike and have plumage consisting of various shades of brown laid down in patterns of stripes, patches, and streaks which make the bird inconspicuous when at rest in a secluded spot in the daytime. The feathers are soft and velvety with furry edges which act as a sound deadening device and the flight feathers are specially adapted for silent flight. This enables the owl to catch its prey unawares and also makes it easier for it to hear the movement of its intended victim.

Because owls are mainly nocturnal, they have large eyes, but these cannot be moved independently of each other, unlike those of other birds. The owl has the ability to turn its head almost right round, in some species as much as 270°, which enables it to change its visual field rapidly. Although each eye has a relatively narrow field of view, the two fields overlap almost completely, giving the bird excellent binocular vision, which enables it to judge distances accurately. It is not true that owls cannot see in daylight, although some species tend to get dazzled in bright sunlight. In absolute darkness, the owl is blind, just as humans are, but it has excellent vision in normal daylight and dusk.

The position of the ears and their structure make for very acute hearing. It should be mentioned that the external 'ears' previously referred to have no connection with the bird's real ears. With this excellent development the owl is able to locate exactly the direction from which the sound of its prey is coming and so more readily obtain its food. Here again, the ability to turn its head round helps in locating the origin of the sound.

Right, Plate 49   A Mackinder's Eagle-Owl *Bubo capensis* stares down from its perch in school-masterly fashion.
Left   The large yellow eyes of Verreaux's Eagle-Owl are specially adapted for its nocturnal feeding habits.

Most owls hunt by night though others are active at dusk and a few in full daylight. They can therefore be regarded as nocturnal counterparts of the diurnal birds-of-prey (Falconiformes), but the two groups are not closely related. Owls have curved, sharp claws on powerful feet and a strong, hooked bill, which enables them to prey on a large range of animals varying in size from an insect to a small deer. Their principal food consists of rodents such as mice and rats but they will also eat other small mammals besides earthworms, reptiles, birds, crabs and even fish.

Occurring only in Africa and Asia, there are seven species of fishing owls, four of which are confined to the latter continent. Although Africa as a whole has three, all belonging to the genus *Scotopelia*, East Africa has only one representative, Pel's Fishing Owl *S. peli*, the largest of the three. Fishing owls catch their prey by snatching it from the surface of the water with their talons, and their feet are cleverly adapted for the purpose. The tarsi are devoid of feathers and the long, sharp, curved claws are lined underneath with numerous spiky scales to grip the wriggling, slippery fish.

Unlike the diurnal birds-of-prey owls do not have a crop, which is normally for food storage during the digestive process, and therefore the prey, swallowed whole, enters the stomach. Digested material is eventually voided in the normal way, but the indigestible matter consisting of fur, feathers, bone and chitin is regurgitated in the form of large pellets some hours later. This process is not uncommon among birds, but the study of owl pellets is particularly valuable in accurately recording their diet, as they cannot digest bones, unlike some species such as herons, which have a stronger digestion. Barn owl pellets collected by the writer have been the subject of an important study at the National Museum in Nairobi.

The majority of owls are arboreal in their habits, but some live among rocks, open grasslands, marshes and even deserts. Only a few species migrate, the Scops Owl *Otus scops* and the Short-eared Owl *Asio flammeus* being the two examples in East Africa.

Breeding is not seasonal, but appears to be based on the availability of the food supply, particularly in those species which prey on rodents. This factor also has a bearing on the number of eggs laid, which may vary tremendously from one to fourteen. Some owls use old nests of other birds, others nest in holes in trees, walls or rocks, and still others on open ground or even in artificial sites provided by human habitations.

The female usually incubates starting with the first egg. In a large clutch, often laid at intervals of as much as forty-eight hours, there is a tremendous difference in size between the youngest and the oldest chicks, the former being in serious danger of being trampled on or eaten by the older ones. The incubation period is long, anything from twenty-five to thirty-five days, depending on the species. Both parents take care of the young which, when born, are blind and covered with down.

Mackinder's Eagle-Owl *Bubo capensis*

With its mottled plumage of orangy-brown, buff and white, fiery orange eyes and prominent 'ear' tufts this is a striking-looking bird of the genus *Bubo*. It is rather thickset and large (22 inches), like other eagle-owls.

It is a high altitude species, not infrequent on Mount Kenya and the Aberdare range where it inhabits rocky crags and cliffs. It is also found in Tanzania. It hunts almost exclusively by night and hides away in crevices during the day. Its call is a resonant hoot.

Below The young of the Spotted Eagle-Owl *Bubo africanus* with their almost-white fluffy feathers.
Bottom Pearl-spotted Owlets *Glaucidium perlatum*, amongst the smallest of the owls, are seen in daylight more often than other owls, when they are liable to be mobbed by various small birds.

24 Kingfishers

The ninety or so species of Kingfishers (family Alcedinidae) divided into three sub-families, are found throughout most of the world, but the great majority are found in the tropical parts of the Old World. One sub-family is fish-eating, another consists of kingfishers which live mainly on insects, often far from water, and the third is made up of fishing and terrestrial-feeding species. All members of the family show distinctive similarities.

Most kingfishers are brilliantly coloured, and are readily identifiable with their large heads and short necks set on compact, powerful bodies. The straight, long bill is generally red and often pointed. Its structure would appear to be an adaptation for fishing, but the fact that tree kingfishers have the same kind of bill belies this. The fish is not speared, but grasped between the mandibles. The short legs are brightly coloured, and some of the toes are fused together for part of their length, a modification to enable the bird to shovel out soil during nest building.

Kingfishers are mainly solitary, although some species are found in small flocks. They habitually perch on branches or stumps, and have a direct rapid flight. Fish-eating birds plunge headlong into water either from a waterside perch or when on the wing. The bird spies its prey, dives into the water with its eyes closed and comes up immediately with or without its catch. Ten plunges are average for a single catch. Small fish are swallowed in flight, larger ones being carried to a perch where they are crushed by beating against a branch and then swallowed headfirst. Besides fish, these kingfishers may take water insects and crustacea; terrestrial species live mainly on large insects.

Kingfishers nest in holes, either in river banks, or for the tree species, in termite nests or tree cavities. The initial depression is made by the bird flying at the bank continuously, attacking it with its beak. Having formed a shallow hole, the kingfisher clings to its edge and begins tunnelling. Soil is loosened by the beak and shovelled out by the specially adapted feet. Depending on the soil, a short or long tunnel is made, which opens out into an unlined nest chamber. The floor of this is soon covered with pellets, which are regurgitations of fish bones and scales. Depending on the species, two to seven white eggs are laid and incubated by both sexes. The hatched young are generally naked and quite helpless.

Left Before swallowing this fish, the Giant Kingfisher will break its bones by battering it against the tree-trunk.

The darkening of the nest as an adult enters stimulates a young bird to open its mouth, in which the small fish is put head first. The satisfied chick then moves away to make room for the next. The young eject liquid faeces into the tunnel, which soon becomes fouled, and the adults have to bathe frequently to clean their feathers. When fledged, the young are dependent on their parents for some time; the art of catching fish, though inherent, has to be perfected with much practice. Many young die due to the repeated wetting, either because of the cold water, or because their feathers become water-logged and they drown.

Giant Kingfisher *Ceryle maxima*

This shy, wary bird is not common anywhere, and is usually found singly or in pairs near wooded streams and rivers. A large bird (about 18 inches), it is readily identifiable by its markedly crested head, chestnut underparts and loud, raucous voice.

It will sit motionless on a branch near water, until a fish appears, when it will plunge straight in without hovering. A small fish is soon killed and swallowed, but I observed a Giant Kingfisher battering a fish almost as big as itself for twenty minutes.

Pied Kingfisher *Ceryle rudis*
When not feeding, this kingfisher is often seen in small flocks and may even nest in colonies. Working from a perch or hovering over the water with rapidly beating wings, this bird will plummet down onto its prey, which seems to be exclusively fish.

About 10 inches long, with a marked crest and conspicuous black and white plumage, this bird is quite fearless. It is often common throughout the Ethiopian Region, both on inland waters and at the coast.

Malachite Kingfisher *Alcedo cristata*
This small bird (5 inches) is unforgettable with its brilliant cobalt-blue, crested head, vivid ultramarine blue underparts, white throat and rich tawny cheeks.

When fishing, it prefers wide waters and swamps with reedy margins, but for breeding it must make its way to a river with high, steep banks in which it can nest. One of the most common kingfishers, it is found locally throughout the Ethiopian Region except Somalia. It is said to feed mainly on fish and aquatic insects.

Opposite top and above Although the Malachite Kingfisher feeds mainly on fish, it also takes frogs and aquatic insects.

Far left to right A Pied Kingfisher returning to its favourite perch, after an unsuccessful dive to catch a fish.

Left, Plate 51 The vivid plumage of a Malachite Kingfisher *Alcedo cristata*.
Below, Plate 52 Giant Kingfisher *Ceryle maxima*.

25 Bee-eaters

There are fifteen species of bee-eaters in East Africa of which one is mainly a migrant from Madagascar, although it is also known to breed on the mainland, and two more are winter migrants from the Palaearctic Region during the non-breeding season. All of the twenty-four members, which make up the family Meropidae, are confined to the Old World.

Bee-eaters are fearless, slim birds and despite some diversity in size, are easily identifiable as members of the same family. The plumage is brilliantly coloured, with green predominating, although yellows, red and blues of various shades also play their part in the colourful pattern. A very common feature is a marked black stripe running back from

Below, Plate 53 Carmine Bee-eater *Merops nubicus*. These birds perch on wild antelopes and domestic animals, and swoop down to take insects flushed by their movements.

the base of the bill through the eye. The tail may be square at the end, or have two elongated central tail feathers or, as in the case of the Swallow-tailed Bee-eater *Merops hirundineus*, be strongly forked. The legs are short with small feet, having part of two of the toes fused as in kingfishers. However, the most characteristic feature is the long, thin, laterally flattened and somewhat down-curved bill, ending in a sharp point.

As its name suggests, the bee-eater's food consists mainly of bees, but it will also take wasps, hornets and similar insects on the wing. The prey is caught in the course of short flights made from a perch or sometimes during continuous hawking. In a study carried out in Rhodesia, it was found that of all insects taken by Swallow-tailed, Carmine *M. nubicus* and other bee-eaters, eighty per cent consisted of the ordinary honey bee *Apis mellifora*. Although the birds have a high immunity to bee venom, it is necessary for them to use a special technique to catch such dangerous insects. The bee is caught in flight between the two mandibles at the tip of the bill. Back on the perch, the bee-eater expertly changes its grip so that the bee is now held near the end of its abdomen where the sting is. The head is knocked vigorously against a branch a number of times until all the venom is discharged. A couple more smart raps on the head and the now harmless bee is ready for swallowing. Bee-eaters are found in all types of country but being arboreal, some tree cover is necessary, although telegraph poles and wire provide a good substitute nowadays. The majority of species are gregarious and are found swooping about in open country, making their trilling call as they fly; but a few of them, such as the Swallow-tailed Bee-eater, are mostly solitary, shy and unobtrusive, preferring forests and woodland areas. The presence of bee-eaters near water is significant only in that insects tend to congregate there, but otherwise the bird needs little water, if any at all.

Most bee-eaters breed colonially and provide a brilliant spectacle as they wheel, bank, flutter and glide near the nesting colony in their hundreds or sometimes even, thousands. Tunnels are dug, the ends of which are expanded into an oval nesting chamber. In a bank, quite often near a river, the burrow is made more or less horizontally, its length varying from two to seven feet. Less frequently the nest is made in flat ground, in which case a short vertical entry passage is excavated and then turned to run parallel to the ground. The nest

Top right The Little Bee-eater *Merops pusillus*, as its name suggests, is perhaps the smallest bee-eater found in Africa, being 6 inches long.
Below and below right Two young White-throated Bee-eaters clamouring for food, and being fed by the adult.

cavity is unlined, but the eggs are protected by a gradually thickening carpet of disintegrating pellets consisting of indigestible parts of insects, ejected by the adults.

Both sexes help to excavate the nest, incubate the two to five eggs and tend the young, which are quite naked when hatched. Even when fledged they need the care and attention of parents, as they must learn from experience, sometimes painful, the technique of catching bees without being stung.

The feeding of the young, at least of the White-throated Bee-eater *Merops albicollis*, is not necessarily left exclusively to the parents as was observed by J. F. Reynolds (1974), who noted the occurrence of 'co-operative breeding', in which a pair of breeding birds is assisted by a number of 'helpers', usually the male offspring of the bird's previous breeding season.

Carmine Bee-eater *Merops nubicus*
A beautiful bird of generally carmine colour, with head and throat of dark greenish-blue and a pale blue rump, it measures 14 inches in length including its elongated central tail feathers. Both sexes are alike.

It frequents coastal bush, savanna regions and arid country in suitable areas in East Africa and is common at the Kenya coast between November and April. It is gregarious and noisy as it nests in large numbers often exceeding a thousand birds. Unlike most other bee-eaters its main diet consists of locusts, grasshoppers and other large insects, and to help obtain these it has developed a special association with animals and large terrestrial birds. It perches on domestic animals such as goats, sheep and cattle, wild antelopes, and large birds such as ostrich and bustard, swooping down on the insects flushed by their movements. It is also attracted to bush fires where it can feed on escaping insects.

White-fronted Bee-eater *Merops bullockoides*
This bird has a square, not elongated tail. Its upper parts are green, the breast and abdomen golden-brown, with bright carmine below the throat and vivid ultramarine tail coverts.

It is a local resident, found in the savanna lands of East and Central Africa, and inhabits dry ravines and banks of rivers.

26 Rollers

In East Africa the order Coraciiformes is represented by some attractive and diverse families, consisting as it does of kingfishers, bee-eaters, hoopoes, wood-hoopoes, hornbills and rollers. Of these the rollers run the kingfishers a very close second in their beauty. The family Coraciidae is a small one, confined to the warmer areas of the Old World, its sixteen members being divided into two genera. Seven of these species occur in tropical Africa, the European Roller *Coracias garrulus* being a Palaearctic migrant. Two other species have a restricted range, the Racquet-tailed Roller *C. spatulata* occurring in Tanzania and Southern Africa and the Blue-throated Roller *Eurystomus gularis* in Uganda and West Africa.

Left, Plate 54 White-fronted Bee-eaters *Merops bullockoides*. These birds have developed a special technique of knocking their poisonous prey against a branch, to release the venom, before eating.
Below, Plate 55 Lilac-breasted Roller *Coracias caudata*. During courtship displays, this colourful bird performs brilliant aerobatics.

Rollers perform brilliant aerobatics during their courtship displays, when they somersault and roll spectacularly in the air, earning them their popular name. However, their loud and raucous cry as they carry out these manoeuvres, seems out of accord with their flashing elegance. They are stoutly built birds of brilliant plumage, with a large head on a short neck. The slightly hooked bill is strong, as are their wings, and the longish tail may be square or forked. The sexes are alike.

Usually found singly or in pairs, and in small loose groups only when migrating, they perch conspicuously on a high vantage point such as a bare branch, telegraph pole or an ant-hill, from which they make sorties to the ground, when they spot a large insect or a lizard. They must have very good eyesight as they are almost always among the first birds to reach a grass fire or a new hatch of termites.

Not a great deal is known about their nesting habits. The three to five eggs are laid in a hole in a tree, bank or rock, the nest having little or no lining. The young are naked when hatched and are looked after by both parents.

Lilac-breasted Roller *Coracias caudata*
Tawny-brown on top, rich lilac on throat and breast, with the remaining plumage of various shades of bright blue or greenish-blue, this roller is perhaps the most attractive of them all. It behaves in a typical roller fashion with its aerobatics, perching habits and harsh call. It is locally common in woodland and open bush country throughout East Africa and often seen during the winter in the same areas as the European Roller.

The European Roller is a common migrant often seen in the same area as the Lilac-breasted Roller. It, too, somersaults and displays during the breeding season.

27 Hornbills

Of the forty-four members of the family Bucerotidae living in the tropical parts of the Old World twenty resident species occur in East Africa and seven of them are only found in Uganda. Hornbills inhabit all types of wooded country, either rainforest, open forest or acacia woodlands. They are noisy and hence conspicuous being found in plentiful numbers in suitable habitats.

They range from medium to large in size, with a moderately long tail in most species, but their most prominent and distinctive feature is the unusually large, generally down-curved bill, often surmounted by a large casque. The toucans of the New World also have enormous bills, but they are in no way related to the Old World hornbills. They have very large mandibles and the presence of the casque gives an impression of a top-heavy bird, liable to tip over on to its head; but these appendages are extremely light as a rule, having a horny shell filled with supporting network of loose, delicate and spongelike bone tissue. The plumage of both sexes is alike in many species, but the bill in the male is often quite different from that of the female, the casque tending to be much smaller in the latter. The legs are short and stout and the structure of the wings is responsible for the loud rushing noise, compared to the 'roar of a train' made by the larger species when in flight.

Hornbills feed on a great variety of fruit and berries, insects, small mammals, reptiles and even birds; the larger species tend to be fruit eaters, whereas some of the smaller ones may be mainly insectivorous.

Their breeding habits were little known until the Moreaus carried out their fine study of the Silvery-cheeked Hornbill *Bycanistes brevis* at Amani in Tanzania over thirty-five years ago. Then late in the 1960s Joan and Alan Root produced their fascinating film, 'The Baobab Tree', which featured a complete and intimate sequence of the nesting of a pair of Red-billed Hornbills *Tockus erythrorynchus* at Tsavo National Park in Kenya, photographed through a window cut into the back of the nest. The large Silvery-cheeked Hornbill *Bycanistes brevis*, about 30 inches long, is found in forests at the coast and in the highlands of East Africa, where it lives on tops of trees in pairs or small parties, except when it roosts communally when it may number up to 150.

The female Silvery-cheeked Hornbill finds a suitable hole or hollow in a tree, generally quite high up, and then proceeds to wall herself in. The male supplies the material which

The large casque of the Silvery-cheeked Hornbill is regarded by some authorities as a resonance chamber for its calls.

consists mainly of earth mixed with viscid mucus and which is regurgitated to the female in the form of pellets. These are patted into the entrance hole until the opening is reduced to a narrow vertical slit. The fact that it is the female that builds the wall indicates that she is not the unwilling prisoner of the male. She continues to leave the nest after work until one day the opening is too small. She then settles down and lays one or two eggs. They hatch in about forty-five days, and during the incubation period she moults. A further sixty days or so elapse before the young are ready to leave the nest. During this entire three and a half months, the male conscientiously feeds, first the sitting female, and then the entire family with fruits, regurgitated and fed in through the slit one by one; he may bring as many as 24,000 fruits in one nesting season. When the young are grown, the female breaks down the wall and the whole family flies away together.

Below A pair of Ground Hornbills preening their feathers after a dust bath.
Bottom, Plate 56 A pair of Ground Hornbills *Bucorvus cafer* in courting display. These are the largest of the hornbills.
Right, Plate 57 Red-billed Hornbill *Tockus erythrorhynchus*. During the breeding season, the female will be walled into the nest hole for many weeks, being fed by the male through an opening.

The ground hornbills *Bucorvus* species are the only members of the family in which the female is not walled in. These are the largest (42 inches) hornbills, resembling a domestic turkey in appearance, but not in taste! They can generally be seen in open savanna country in family parties of two to eight, quartering their territory on foot, looking for food. Nests made in hollow trees or stumps and occasionally in small caves in a cliff face, are used year after year. The female lays one or two eggs, does not moult, and is therefore still able to fly during the incubation period. She may leave the nest from time to time at this stage to search for food, but is also fed at the nest. The young take eighty to eighty-five days to fledge and then remain with the parents for a considerable time.

Red-billed Hornbill *Tockus erythrorhynchus*

This is a smaller hornbill (18 inches), mostly black and white in colour, with a red bill, conspicuous in semi-desert districts by its monotonous and continuous 'tok-tok-tok-tok' call. It is one of the most common hornbills found in acacia woodlands.

It nests in natural holes in trees, the opening being walled up by the female with a mixture of mud, dung and saliva, generally but not invariably brought to her by the male, until a slit opening remains through which the latter feeds her. Three to six eggs are laid and during incubation the female moults.

The speed of moulting seems to bear some relationship to the problem of feeding the young. In the small, mainly insectivorous hornbills, the moult is very quick and the female grows the feathers again equally rapidly. This enables her to break out, when the young are only half-grown, to help her mate in feeding the family still in the nest. This happens in the case of the Red-billed Hornbill and the young have the quite remarkable ability to repair the damaged exit by replastering with dung etc., as soon as the female has left. Both parents are needed to find the necessary insect food, rapidly depleting as the relatively short rainy season ends, to feed the many voracious young. In the larger, frugivorous species, with only one or two young, and with a much more prolonged and readily available food supply, the male can cope with all the food requirements and the female moults slowly and does not leave the nest cavity until the young are also ready to fly.

Ground Hornbill *Bucorvus cafer*

The habits of this hornbill, which is closely related to the Abyssinian Ground Hornbill *B. abyssinicus* have already been described earlier in this chapter. Its plumage is generally black, and the skin of its face and throat is red in the male and generally blue in the female.

28 Barbets

At a superficial glance barbets might be mistaken for woodpeckers and this would be understandable as the two families are related. Both make nest holes and some barbets even have the ability to climb trees in the manner of woodpeckers; but these strongly built, colourful birds, with their compact bodies and stout, heavy, sharply pointed bills are members of the family Capitonidae. They are typical birds of the tropic areas of America, Africa and Asia, each continent having its own species; but they are more abundant in Africa than in any other part of the world. In East Africa alone there are thirty species, of which three are found only in Tanzania and four in Uganda. Their sizes range from the 3½ inches of the Red-fronted Tinker-bird *Pogoniulus pusillus* to the 9 inches of some members of the genus *Trachyphonus*. Their family name is derived from the well-developed tufts of bristles around the nostrils and on the chin. In most species, both sexes are alike.

Barbets are primarily forest birds, but some like to live in sparsely wooded areas and a few have adapted to live in savanna and even semi-arid areas. Although mostly fruit and seed eaters, a partial or a predominant diet of insects has been adopted by some species in savanna country. Although barbets normally live singly or in pairs, they are often found in large numbers in trees which are in fruit, particularly the wild fig *Ficus* species.

Most barbets spend their time sitting high up in a tree, monotonously producing a single note of a shrill, metallic quality, over and over again without ceasing. They nest in holes, most of them in dead trees, but some species nest in the ground. It may therefore be convenient to divide them into two groups, the former being known as 'tree' barbets, and the latter, being three members of the genus *Trachyphonus*, as 'ground' barbets. The fourth member of this genus, like the other three, feeds on termites and other ground insects, but makes its nest hole in a tree.

An entrance hole, just wide enough to give access to one bird at a time, is started by a tree-nesting barbet on the underside of a sloping, dead or decaying branch. A tunnel is built which runs along the length of the branch and opens out into the nesting chamber.

Top right A Red-and-Yellow Barbet on a thorn tree, typical of the habitat it frequents.
Centre right A Spotted-flanked Barbet *Lybius lacrymosus* busy excavating a hole in a tree which it may use for roosting or nesting.
Bottom right, Plate 59 Red-and-Yellow Barbet *Trachyphonus erythrocephalus*. This barbet also has a typical display and call.
Below The entrance hole to the nest of a D'Arnaud's Barbet, situated near a small bush.
Bottom, Plate 58 The D'Arnaud's Barbet *Trachyphonus darnaudii* has a characteristic call, and males and females can be seen singing duets and displaying to each other.

Of the three ground nesting barbets, the Red-and-Yellow Barbet *T. erythrocephalus* and the Yellow-breasted Barbet *T. margaritatus* dig their tunnel in a steep bank, a termite mound or in the wall of a pit. D'Arnaud's Barbet *T. darnaudii* on the other hand, selects a level piece of sandy ground in which it tunnels a vertical shaft, anything up to 36 inches long, which turns laterally and then slightly upwards into the enlarged nesting chamber, to prevent it being flooded by rain.

Two to five eggs are laid on a layer of wood chips or other vegetation and both parents incubate. The young are born naked and blind and remain in the nest for some period, maybe as long as four to five weeks; and after, remaining with the parents for some months.

Parasitic honeyguides (Indicatoridae) are known to make frequent use of the African barbets as unwitting foster-parents.

D'Arnaud's Barbet *Trachyphonus darnaudii*
Red-and-Yellow Barbet *Trachyphonus erythrocephalus*
Both these ground species frequent open thornbush areas and semi-arid or arid bush country, the latter preferring localities where there are termite hills in which it can breed. Both are striking looking birds, the Red-and-Yellow Barbet being the larger (9 inches) and having, as its name implies, red and yellow plumage, whereas D'Arnaud's Barbet is 6 inches long, with its yellow colour mixed with brown and orange. Both have round white spots on the wings.

Both species have unmistakable and characteristic calls, though different, uttered either in the form of a duet or sometimes in a chorus of several birds. The display which accompanies these songs has been remarked on by a number of observers. Sir Frederick Jackson records that the Red-and-Yellow Barbets 'seem to work themselves up into a great state of excitement and perform many curious antics', and R. E. Moreau has studied the display of the D'Arnaud's Barbet in great detail. There is little difference in the antics of the two species, but the suggestion that this communal display may be confined to the three ground barbets of the genus *Trachyphonus* may well have to be revised. The writer has often observed in his garden a resident pair of White-headed Barbets *Lybius leucocephalus* singing a duet and displaying.

29 Swallows

Swallows belong to the family Hirundinidae, of which martins are also members. As there is little significant difference between the two species, martins are commonly included under the general term 'swallow'. A distinction should be made, however, between swallows and swifts; although swifts live in a similar environment and physically resemble swallows, they belong to a quite different taxonomic order.

The family Hirundinidae has an almost worldwide distribution, its seventy-four or so member-species being found at all altitudes and in all types of country. They are small, slender birds, and have a small bill with a wide gape. The tail is usually forked, and short, although in some cases the main outer tail feathers are considerably elongated. They have short legs and weak feet, but their long, pointed wings enable them to fly swiftly for long periods, showing remarkable manoeuvrability in the air.

Their diet consists entirely of insects taken on the wing, a fact which forces them to migrate from temperate to warm climates during the winter months. The migration of swallows has been known for a long time, reference being made to it in the Bible. The birds often travel great distances, and as they are gregarious they form very large groups for their journey in autumn. The best-known of these migrants is the European Swallow *Hirundo rustica*. Widely distributed and equally well-known in Africa is the Striped Swallow *Hirundo abyssinica*, which is readily recognized by its chestnut crown and rump, black-streaked underparts and the thin and elongated outer tail feathers. Its call sounds like a rusty hinge in need of oiling.

The swallow spends most of its time on the wing and can perch on wires etc., only alighting on the ground to collect mud for nest-building. The differences in their nesting habits may indicate their evolutionary progress. The most primitive use unlined natural holes in trees and banks; others, including rough-winged swallows, make tunnels which lead to lined chambers, in banks or level ground. The most advanced species construct nests of mud which range in shape from open saucer-shaped structures to sophisticated chambers with tunnel entrances. Three to seven eggs are laid, which are incubated by both parents. The parents also feed the young in the nest for three or more weeks.

Red-rumped Swallow *Hirundo daurica*

There are twelve sub-species of this swallow, which are found throughout southern Europe, southern Asia and central Africa. Although they sometimes make their nests in buildings, this species tends to inhabit wild regions. In Africa, they are found in wooded savanna country, particularly where escarpments provide suitable sites for nests. These birds are known to migrate locally, although the pattern and extent of this movement has not been clearly established.

The Red-rumped Swallow is closely related to the Mosque Swallow *H. senegalensis* and differs from it in appearance by being smaller (7 inches) and having black undertail coverts instead of rufous. Otherwise the upper parts are blue-black with contrasting rufous rumps and pale rufous underparts in both species. The tail is forked.

The nest is made of mud and plastered to an overhanging projection in a building or cave. It is retort-shaped with a side tunnel entrance. Two or three eggs are laid.

Below left A pair of Striped Swallows collect mud for nest-building from a puddle, until their cheeks bulge.
Below and Bottom The mud, mixed with saliva, is squeezed out of the mouth in the form of a paste which is then tapped into position by the beak, and soon hardens.
Right, Plate 60 Red-rumped Swallows *Hirundo daurica*.

30 Pipits and Longclaws

Pipits, longclaws and wagtails are all members of the family Motacillidae. In East Africa the family is represented by twenty-four species consisting of six wagtails, thirteen pipits and five longclaws. Three species each of pipits and wagtails are Palaearctic migrants; the only longclaw in Uganda is the Yellow-throated *Macronyx croceus*; and Sharpe's Longclaw *Macronyx sharpei* is endemic to Kenya, occurring in the highlands over 7000 feet. Their range extends from sea level to high mountains.

Pipits and larks predominate on the open grasslands of Africa, and although somewhat alike in appearance, the two families are not closely related, the latter being members of the Alaudidae. The family under discussion consists of graceful and slender birds, with an upright stance and generally with slender bills and long tails. They are mainly terrestrial in habit, and only a few species commonly perch on trees or bushes.

Birds of this family have strong feet, a particular feature being the relatively long toes, the hind claw being much elongated. The longest toes are found in the longclaws; in the Yellow-throated, the hind claw is nearly two inches in length and the total length of the foot may be as long as three and a half inches. This is another resemblance to the larks. Pipits and wagtails are mainly insectivorous, living on various insects which inhabit grassy areas, such as flies, beetles and grasshoppers, but they will also eat small seeds.

The nest is usually a well-made cup of grass, lined with finer material, built on the ground among tufts of grass, and is generally protected and well-hidden. The two to four eggs are incubated by the female or sometimes by both sexes. The newly hatched young are naked but covered with down on the upper parts. Both parents feed the chicks.

Rosy-breasted Longclaw *Macronyx amerliae*
This is a sturdy pipit, 8 inches long, with streaky brown upperparts, bright salmon-red underparts and a black chest band. Although widespread, it is not common anywhere. It prefers to inhabit swampy areas of grass-land and is very eye-catching.

The nest is typical, built on a grass hummock in a swampy area, and somewhat above ground level to prevent flooding. Van Someren (1956) estimates an incubation period of thirteen to fourteen days and a fledging period of about sixteen days.

Left The characteristic upright stance of the graceful Plain-backed Pippit *Anthus leucophrys*.
Above, Plate 61 Rosy-breasted Longclaw *Macronyx amerliae*. This is an eye-catching bird, with its salmon-red underparts and black chest bands.
Right A Wagtail *Motacilla alba* which belongs to the same family as pipits and longclaws.

31 Shrikes

The family of shrikes (Laniidae) is widespread but confined to the Old World. About seventy members make up the world family, of which fifty are found in East Africa, four of these being Palaearctic migrants. A diverse group, the family's main characteristic is the hook at the tip of the upper mandible, behind which is a 'tooth' which fits into a corresponding notch on the lower mandible. These birds have well-developed rictal bristles, strong legs with sharp claws designed to grasp prey, and plumage varying from predominantly black and white to extremely colourful.

Shrikes are essentially carnivorous, their diet consisting mainly of insects although some species supplement this by eating young birds, eggs and small mammals. Although the family is divided into four sub-families, there is some uncertainty as to the relationship between the species, and their classification.

True Shrikes (sub-family Laniinae) are perhaps the most typical of the family, widely distributed in Europe, Asia and Africa. Members of the genus *Lanius* have robust bills, strongly hooked, with a well-marked 'tooth' and notch. They are bold and aggressive birds, the larger species taking small mammals and reptiles as well as insects. They plunge down to the ground to catch their prey, or take insects on the wing. The habit of impaling their prey on thorns and barbed wire or wedging them in forks of branches, which earns them the popular name 'butcher bird', is more common in countries where an unfavourable climate may make the provision of a 'larder' a distinct advantage.

The Fiscal Shrike *Lanius collaris*, with its strongly contrasted black-and-white plumage, is a common bird in Africa. Being strongly territorial, they will fiercely drive away other birds they regard as intruders or enemies. They are undoubtedly successful breeders, despite the fact that their open, cup-shaped nests, built of twigs, grasses, etc., are placed visibly on an open branch, and are thus vulnerable to predation. They seem to rely on their bold and aggressive nature to drive off unwelcome visitors, though they find the larger raptors such as kites, eagles and crows impossible to oppose successfully. The Fiscal Shrikes seem to tolerate other species in their vicinity, giving an occasional show of strength.

Left The Red-tailed Shrike *Lanius cristatus* is a common winter visitor to East Africa.
Right The Fiscal Shrike *Lanius collaris* at its nest observed by its expectant offspring.

Bush Shrikes. This is a wholly African sub-family (Malaconotinae) and is much less homogeneous than the true shrikes. The bill may vary from moderately weak to strong, and the 'tooth' and notch are less marked. The plumage is sometimes entirely black as in the Sooty Boubou *Laniarius poensis*; in some cases the underparts are brightly coloured, for example, Gonoleks; but most colourful are the members of the genus *Malaconotus*, such as the Many-coloured Bush Shrike *M. multicolor* and the Black-fronted Bush Shrike *M. nigrifrons*. These display a number of colour phases, each more striking than the last. Members of this sub-family are generally difficult to observe as they tend to confine themselves to forests.

Most species have a distinctive call, some of them quite musical and melodious. Special mention must be made of the duet singing of the male and female, especially of the Tropical Boubou, *Laniarius aethiopicus*. Each pair of birds seems to have a distinctive repertoire, each member with its own part. The first part of the song, sung by one of the pair, is so promptly followed by the second member that it sounds like a solo.

Unlike the true shrikes, the bush shrikes hide their cup-shaped nests in thick foliage or dense undergrowth.

Helmet shrikes. Another exclusively African sub-family (Prionopinae) is characterized by the extreme sociability of its members, which are generally found in small parties, even during nesting time. They are entirely insectivorous, and are said to help each other to build a nest and even to feed the young.

Rueppell's White-crowned Shrike *Eurocephalus rueppelli*
This is a helmet shrike whose relationship with other shrikes is not clearly established. It is believed that this genus contains two species, one confined to southern Africa, and the above, which ranges as far as Ethiopia in Eastern Africa.

The White-crowned Shrike is about 9 inches long with an ashy brown mantle, contrasting white crown, lower and upper tail coverts and rump, and a wide black patch behind the eye. They are usually found in small parties of up to twelve members, and have a characteristic butterfly-like flight as they glide, stiff-winged, from tree to tree in search of food. This bird builds an amazingly compact nest, neatly made of various materials woven over with spiders' webs. Two or three eggs are laid, but two hens often lay in the same nest.

Plate 62 Rueppell's White-crowned Shrike *Eurocephalus rueppelli*. These sociable birds are said to help each other build nests, and even feed the young.

32 Babblers

Mackworth-Praed and Grant (1955) considered babblers, combined with chatterers, as part of the family Turdodidae in Eastern Africa. More recently, however, it is preferred to regard them as a sub-family of the large family Muscicapidae, which also includes thrushes, flycatchers, warblers and other mainly insectivorous birds. This sub-family is divided into two tribes, of which the Turdoidini is represented in the Ethiopian Region by fourteen species divided into two genera. The monotypic Capuchin Babbler *Phyllanthus atripennis* is only found in Uganda and the remaining ten species belong to the genus *Turdoides*, which contains two East African endemic species, Hinde's Pied Babbler *Turdoides hindei* being confined only to Kenya and the Northern Pied Babbler *T. hypoleucus* which lives in Kenya and Tanzania. At the present time there is some doubt about the status of the former.

Babblers are thrush-like, raucous birds, keeping up a continuous chatter as they move around in noisy parties in bush country, looking for food, consisting mainly of insects and a little fruit, amongst bushes or on the ground. Their plumage is usually dull, brown, rufous or grey in colour and the sexes are alike.

Northern Pied Babbler *Turdoides hypoleucus*

A stocky, typical babbler about 9 inches long, with a greyish-brown back, white underparts and a conspicuous dark patch on each side of the chest, it is said to occur locally in acacia country in southern Kenya and northern Tanzania. In recent years, it has colonized gardens, not only on the outskirts of Nairobi, the capital of Kenya, but has cultivated areas much nearer the centre of town and a group of four was once observed babbling and proceeding from bush to bush in the very heart of the city!

During 1973, it was possible for the writer to observe four nests of this species in his garden, during which period two complete observations were made, starting from the laying of the eggs to the flying away of the young. The nest in each case was made of a cup of coarse grass, lined with finer grass. In one case the nest was made in a Kei Apple *Aberia caffra* hedge and in the other three instances it was built in a *Cupressus arizonica* hedge. All four nests were situated in the middle of the hedge about five feet from the ground and twelve inches from the top.

One nest contained two eggs and on the other three occasions there were three. The incubation period was found to be sixteen to seventeen days and the young left the nest at fifteen to sixteen days.

Left The Black-lored Babbler *Turdoides melanops* is found in noisy parties usually near water in acacia country.
Above, Plate 63 Northern Pied Babbler *Turdoides hypoleucus*. As its name implies, this is a noisy bird found in large, raucous parties.

33 *Paradise Flycatchers*

The family Muscicapidae is a very large one, consisting as it does of nearly 1400 species. In East Africa it is represented by some 260 members, divided into six sub-families, and reference has already been made to the sub-family of babblers in the previous chapter. The sub-family Monarchinae is represented by twelve species in East Africa and, in this chapter, we are particularly concerned with members of its genus *Terpsiphone*, known as paradise flycatchers. The elongated colourful tail feathers of the male somewhat resemble the decorative plumes of the true Bird of Paradise, but the birds are not related.

The paradise flycatchers, which consist of about eleven species, are found in almost all the tropical countries of the Old World, but are most common in Africa south of the Sahara. The two East African species, the Black-headed Paradise Flycatcher *T. rufiventer* also known as the Red-bellied Paradise Flycatcher and the African Paradise Flycatcher *T. viridis* are found in all the three territories, Kenya, Uganda and Tanzania.

In Africa and Asia most of the males of the same species show considerable variations in the colour of their plumage; the various species also tend to hybridize where their ranges overlap, so there is considerable divergence amongst taxonomists about their status. Some species also carry out seasonal local migrations which confuse the issue still further. The more widespread of the two Asian species, the Asiatic Paradise Flycatcher *T. paradisi*, is the largest of all flycatchers and is frequently found in its white form.

African Paradise Flycatcher *Terpsiphone viridis*

Both sexes of this species are about the same size (8 inches) in the non-breeding season, but during the breeding season, the two central tail feathers in the male are considerably elongated and the bird has a length of up to 14 inches. These long feathers are later lost in moult. Unusually, the male has been known to breed when a year old, even though it lacks the long tail. It is a most colourful bird, readily identified in the field. With its combination of glossy-black chest, neck and head, blue eye-ring and bill, chestnut back, wings and tail, and black flight feathers, it is unmistakable. In some parts of its distribution, particularly along the coast, it is more common in its white or partial white phase, when in the adult male the tail, back and wings are white. The female does not acquire white plumage.

Their food consists of insects, sometimes surprisingly large ones such as dragonflies, caught on the wing in typical flycatcher fashion. The birds perch on a branch and make sudden sorties, the male particularly providing a delightful spectacle with its flamboyant flight, the long tail feathers fluttering conspicuously.

The nest consists of a small, neat cup, usually in the fork of a branch, and is built of twigs, grass and lichen, lined with hair or fine grass. Cobwebs are used in the construction both during the building and to help anchor the nest firmly to the branch. With lichen often decorating its exterior, the nest is remarkably inconspicuous. Its siting, along a thin branch, seems to be of significance against predation by mammals but an overhead canopy of leaves is essential if the young are to survive a sudden tropical downpour. Two or three eggs are laid and the male assists in incubation. It is an absurd sight to see the large bird sitting on a nest hardly two inches across, with its long tail overhanging. As the chicks grow, the nest soon becomes overcrowded particularly if the flycatcher has been victimized by a parasitic Emerald Cuckoo *Chrysococcyx cupreus* as is often the case.

The birds are quite tame during the breeding season. The writer has been able to approach within inches of the nest before flushing the sitting bird. The only reaction shown by this particular pair over an observation period of five days was when a pair of Fiscal Shrikes *Lanius collaris* came near the nest, which by then contained young nestlings. The shrikes were seen off fearlessly by both flycatchers, uttering their characteristic, alarm and anger calls, the chase continuing until the intruders were well away from the nest.

The African Paradise Flycatcher is widespread throughout East Africa and is locally common. It inhabits forests, wooded areas, thick scrub, cultivated areas and gardens, provided they have good tree coverage and heavy undergrowth.

Above and below Although the body size of the male and female African Paradise Flycatcher is the same, the former in its breeding plumage develops a spectacularly long tail.

Right, Plate 64 African Paradise Flycatcher *Terpsiphone viridis*. The magnificent tail feathers of the paradise flycatchers resemble those of the true Birds of Paradise.

34 Sunbirds

Sunbirds of the family Nectariniidae are found throughout the tropical world and exceed 110 species. Of these, the largest number is found in Africa. East Africa alone has fifty species, four of which are endemic, three being confined to Tanzania. Sunbirds occupy a similar niche in the warmer parts of the Old World to that filled by hummingbirds in the New World. Both groups have brilliant plumage and take nectar from flowers, thus helping in their pollination. They are therefore often thought to be related, but their structural similarities are only superficial. Unlike hummingbirds, sunbirds can neither hover while feeding (although they can hang in the air for a few seconds by rapid movements of their wings), nor fly backwards, and the two families are not allied. The fact that some sunbirds pierce the side of the larger, tubular flowers to get at the nectar and so avoid touching the stamens and stigmas, may indicate that their role in pollination is not as significant as that of the hummingbirds.

Sunbirds are a distinct family of small to very small birds, their length being from 4 to 9 inches, with slender pointed, down-curved bills, the male in most species having brilliantly coloured plumage, most of it with an iridescent metallic sheen. The one major exception is the genus *Arachnothera*, with its ten members, commonly known as spiderhunters, found throughout South-east Asia, and which have dull plumage with no bright metallic colour. In spite of their name, the spiderhunters do not feed exclusively on spiders, but will take nectar and small insects in the manner of other sunbirds. The tails of sunbirds are either square or graduated and in some species the two central tail feathers are considerably elongated. The females in most cases are drab, and difficult to identify in the field.

Their flight is very rapid and rather erratic as they move from blossom to blossom, frequently calling in their sharp metallic voices and giving an impression of tremendous activity and restlessness. Sunbirds eat a large quantity of small insects, and also take nectar from tubular flowers, sometimes on the wing, but much more often from a perch. The specially designed tongue enables them to suck up nectar if they can reach it, otherwise they pierce the side of the flower to get at it. They are generally seen singly or in pairs, but often a number, either of the same or of different species, may be seen on the same flowering shrub or tree. They seem particularly attracted to orange or red flowers and their favourite plants include *Aloe*, *Erythrina* and *Leonotis*.

There is some indication of migration, but this is mostly local, conditioned by the flowering seasons of the trees and shrubs on which the birds are dependent for their nutrition. They inhabit all types of country including forests, savanna and cultivated areas, at all altitudes. Some species are restricted to high mountains and others are a familiar sight in gardens at lower heights. The general pattern of their distribution indicates that the duller members are found in dense forests, where they spend most of their lives either in the treetops or close to the ground, the brilliantly-coloured species in more open country.

The sunbirds build a closed nest, generally made of grass, roots, fibres etc., bound together with spiders' webs and suspended from the tip of a branch. It is quite an elaborate structure, usually lined with feathers or down and has a side entrance which may have a projecting porch above it. Both sexes normally build the nest and feed the young, but it is usually the female which incubates the clutch of two or three eggs. In Africa, sunbirds are sometimes parasitized by the smaller cuckoos, such as Klaas's *Chrysococcyx klaas* and the Emerald *C. cupreus*; the expanding size of the young parasite may well burst the nest.

Bronze Sunbird *Nectarinia kilimensis*
The central elongated tail feathers of the male of this species makes it about 9 inches long, whereas the female with its square tail is only 5½ inches in length. The female is drab, olive-grey, but the male shows a metallic bronzy-green iridescence in favourable light; otherwise the general impression is of a purplish-black looking bird. It is very widespread in Kenya and Uganda, often seen in gardens and certainly the most common species in Nairobi gardens. It is generally confined to the highlands being most frequently seen between 5000 and 7000 feet.

The nest is typical, being made of grass, lichen, etc., and covered with spiders' webs. Both sexes feed the usually single young, but the female's feeding trips to the nest may exceed that of the male by as much as ten to one.

Below A typical nest of the Bronzy Sunbird. The female seems to attend to the young far more frequently than the male.
Right, Plate 65 This splendid Bronzy Sunbird *Nectarinia kilimensis* takes nectar from an aloe flower.

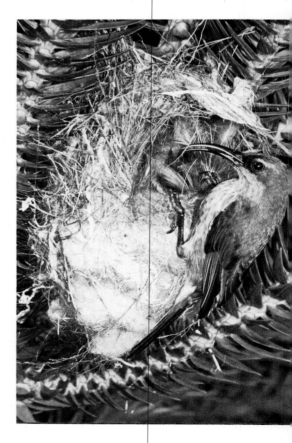

35 Finches

The family Fringillidae is a heterogeneous group which has been divided into a number of sub-families, some authorities recognizing five and others three. However, as far as East Africa is concerned, the discussion is academic as the only sub-family represented is the Carduelinae. Most taxonomists include in the Fringillidae as one of its sub-families, the Geospizinae, consisting of the peculiar group of finches confined to the Galapagos Islands.

Charles Darwin was twenty-six years old, when in 1835 he visited the Galapagos for a period of five weeks on the British survey vessel H.M.S. Beagle. This was a historic occasion as the Islands provided the evidence for his 'Origin of Species', not published until 1859. His interest was first caught by the varied forms of giant tortoises found on different islands. Later he was to appreciate the significance of the finches and was to remark on the diversity of structure and the gradation of sizes in their beaks, and the possibility of the evolution of the different forms from a single species. Even today, finches found elsewhere continue to be a highly interesting group for students of evolution, because of the adaptation of their bills for obtaining seeds from different sources.

Some species feed on fairly readily available seeds, and for this the bill can be quite slender as in the case of the Goldfinch *Carduelis carduelis*. The Hawfinch *Coccothraustes coccothraustes*, on the other hand, has a strong, well-developed bill to enable it to crack very hard nuts or seeds, from which it extracts the kernels. The most curious adaptation of all is perhaps shown by the cross-bill *Loxia* species in which the tip of the mandibles cross to enable the bird to extract seeds from the cones of conifers.

Twigs, grass and roots are used to build the compact cup-shaped nest, only the female carrying out this operation, though the male may be in close attendance. The nest is lined with finer material including down and feathers. Again, only the hen incubates, for a period of ten to fourteen days and the young are fed by regurgitation.

The sub-family Carduelinae consists in East Africa of two genera, *Serinus* having thirteen species and *Linurgus* being monotypic. The serins *Serinus* species are predominantly African, only three of the thirty-one species being found elsewhere. They are arboreal, generally found in open bush or cultivated areas where there are groups of trees, and are often seen feeding on the ground.

Serins are generally good songsters, the pride of place being taken by the Canary *Serinus canaria*, which can be trained to a high musical standard. This ability rather than its appearance (the Goldfinch is much prettier) that has led to its domestication, perhaps the first passerine to have suffered this fate. The wild canary originated from the Canary Islands and is the ancestor of all the domestic canaries. It was introduced into Europe by the Spaniards early in the sixteenth century, and by selective breeding and hybridization, a large number of forms, of different colours and shapes has been produced. A lively trade exists and many a home in Europe is brightened by the eager, whistling and twittering song of the Canary. In Africa, its place seems to be taken by the Yellow-fronted Canary *S. mozambicus*, an equally sweet but less powerful songster.

Streaky Seed-eater *Serinus striolatus*

This is a tawny-brown serin, 6 inches long, striated on the upper parts, crown, throat, breast and flanks and with a distinctively marked white eye-stripe, by which it is readily recognized. It is commonly found in the highlands of East Africa in all kinds of habitat and is a regular visitor to gardens. It has a soft, three-note call and a tinkling canary-like song, rather reminiscent of a bulbul.

Plate 66 The Streaky Seed-eater *Serinus striolatus*, like other serins such as the Canary, is a good songster.

36 Weavers

Certainly in East Africa, the family of weavers (Ploceidae) is the second largest after the Muscicapidae, even after the weaver-finches, previously regarded as belonging to the same family, have been classified separately as Estrildidae, though there is little doubt about their close relationship. Of the world total of 142 species, East Africa has eighty-nine weavers, five of which are endemic. The family is predominantly African.

This group is so varied that a general description of the whole family is not possible, and it is divided into six sub-families, in turn separated into sixteen genera, five being monotypic. They all share the ability to tie a knot and so build a truly woven nest, which is completely enclosed. Weavers start their nests by taking a long piece of grass, which they usually place at the tip of a branch, holding one end down with a foot and then, with the beak, proceeding to work the other end in, out and over, thus fastening it in a knot. This procedure is continued until a suspended ring is formed, providing the basis of the nest. More and more strands are woven in, the bird standing in the middle of the ring, until a hollow ball is made. Each piece of grass in meticulously worked in, the end pulled through and the loose end tucked away.

Some weavers build very elaborate hanging nests, with entrances at the side or at the bottom. Access is gained through a long entrance tunnel hanging down vertically from the globular nest. A safety partition is often provided to prevent the eggs from rolling out, the nest of the Spectacled Weaver *Ploceus ocularis* being a typical example. Perhaps the most handsome nest built by any weaver is that of the bird with a very heavy bill, aptly named the Grosbeak Weaver *Amblyospiza albifrons*. It is fixed between two or three upright stems of reeds, very finely woven and with a small side entrance. To obtain its nesting material the male grasps the edge of a reed frond with its beak and then flies away, thus tearing off a thin thread which is then woven in to make an astonishingly beautiful structure. Other weavers assemble vegetable fibres much more loosely and untidily, but the typical globular or oval shape is maintained.

The Pin-tailed Whydah lays its eggs in the nest of other birds. When the young hatch, they mimic the colour and behaviour patterns of their hosts so as to be fed.

Many species are sociable and breed in loose association or definite colonies. An acacia tree, festooned with nests of the Black-headed Weaver *Ploceus cucullatus* hardly a foot apart, is a hive of noisy activity as the males build, display and chatter during the breeding season. One of the survival techniques used by weavers is the building of hanging nests, sometimes over water, to protect them from predation by monkeys, snakes etc. Other safety devices employed are the positioning of the entrance on the underside; the entry tunnel; the siting at the top of a thin branch and the building of nests very close to habitations of stinging insects, large birds or even human beings.

East African weavers may conveniently be divided into six sub-families: Viduinae – Nest parasitic whydahs and indigo-birds; Ploceinae – True weavers; Bubalornithinae – Buffalo weavers; Plocepasserinae – Sparrow weavers; Passerinae – Sparrows and Petronias and Sporopipanae – Scaly weavers.

Members of the genus *Euplectes* of the true weavers, are also popularly known interchangeably as whydahs or widow-birds. These are distinguished from the parasitic whydahs and indigo birds of the sub-family Viduinae, by referring to the latter as the viduine whydahs or weavers.

Viduine Whydahs. Almost certainly all members of this sub-family are brood parasitic, but much remains to be learnt about their biology. Typical birds of the open plain and savanna, they are widely distributed in Africa south of the Sahara. A common characteristic is the dull, streaked, sparrow-like appearance of the female, the immature male and the male in

This Red-naped Widow-bird may be a female or a male in non-breeding plumage.
Overleaf left, Plate 67 Red-naped Widow-bird *Euplectes ardens*. Only the male develops these remarkable, elongated feathers.
Overleaf right, Plate 68 A male Pin-tailed Whydah *Vidua macroura*. The male hovers and dances over the female during the characteristic courtship ritual.

Plate 70 The Golden Weaver *Ploceus subaureus* nests in noisy breeding colonies, where clusters of well-woven nests can be seen.

the non-breeding plumage. In the breeding season, however, the male becomes predominantly black and in the genus *Vidua* it generally acquires four, equally elongated central tail feathers. These social birds move in flocks and are often seen feeding on small seeds (and rarely insects) on the ground, in company with other weavers and weaver-finches, sometimes even with their specific hosts.

Viduine whydahs are now known to parasitize exclusively members of four genera of weaver-finches, each species of whydah laying its eggs in the nest of a specific host. The Paradise Whydah *Vidua paradisea* parasitizes the nest of the Melba Finch *Pytilia melba*, and Fischer's Whydah *V. fischeri* that of the Purple Grenadier *Uraeginthus ianthinogaster*.

Adult or newly-hatched cuckoos and honey-guides will destroy the eggs or evict the young of their hosts, thus reducing their rate of reproduction, but the young viduine whydahs must compete for food with those of the host. Each member of the weaver-finch family has a very strongly developed sense of what its young should look like. The latter have elaborate, colourful and conspicuous patterns on the gape and palate, differing from one species to the other. The chicks also differ in colour, skin texture and the manner in which they beg for food. In order to compete for food on equal terms with the nestlings of the hosts, the young whydahs mimic their colour patterns and behaviour to an extraordinary degree, with the result that the foster parents are completely taken in and feed the intruders by regurgitations from the crop. Both groups of young are thus reared simultaneously. The adopted youngs' association with their foster family may continue for a considerable period after fledging.

Particularly during the breeding season, the viduine whydahs live in colonies of varying sizes in areas where their hosts reside, with the result that a large number of the nests of the latter may contain the intruders' eggs, as two or three such eggs are generally laid per nest.

True Weavers. Of the ninety-three species of the sub-family Ploceinae all but five are confined to the Ethiopian Region and the neighbouring islands, four of these being endemic in East Africa. Most of them have part of their plumage bright yellow or red. Many eat both seeds and insects, other mainly seeds, and a few are mostly insectivorous. The largest genus, *Ploceus* has thirty-four species, distributed in every kind of arboreal habitat. They have bright yellow in their plumage, build elaborate suspended nests, some with tunnel entrances, and are generally polygamous. They tend to employ the nest protection methods mentioned earlier. The sexes differ considerably in appearance, the female being sparrow-like and the male sometimes assuming this dull plumage during the non-breeding season. During this period the weavers form large wandering flocks.

Of the three members of the genus *Quelea*, perhaps the Red-billed Quelea *Q. quelea* is the most widely known; or rather notorious. It is extremely gregarious and its enormous flocks may number hundreds of thousands. The birds migrate in East Africa to different areas as the grain ripens and cause tremendous damage to wheat and other ripe and ripening crops. The nesting colonies are vast, the nests rapidly built by the males, so close as to almost touch each other. Queleas, unlike many of the true weavers, are monogamous and attract a female to the nest by a characteristic display. Breeding is very rapid, only four weeks being required to cover the incubation and nesting periods.

Because of the immense destruction which they cause to cereals, they are regarded as pests and massive campaigns have been mounted against them. Unfortunately, methods of destroying quelea roosting sites sometimes destroy those of other, inoffensive weavers.

The fifteen species of the sub-family Euplectes consist of bishops and non-parasitic widow-birds or whydahs. Their globular nests are not so specialized, being placed in grass

or low vegetation instead of suspended from trees, and consequently do not have the same degree of protection as those of the genus *Ploceus*. The males of the bishops in the breeding dress are glossy black, with some brilliant red or yellow plumage and a short tail. Widow-bird males have less brilliant colouring, but the tails are elongated and elaborate and in the case of the Long-tailed Widow-bird *E. progne*, which has the longest tail of all this group, the length of the bird increases by 8 to 14 inches in its nuptial plumage, entirely due to the lengthening of the tail feathers.

All the females are very much alike, again being streaky and dull, and the males also have a similar non-breeding plumage. Bishops and widow-birds are polygamous and many males have four to six females nesting at any one time. This, combined with the fact that they do not nest on trees, makes them highly territorial, and the male is kept busy patrolling his boundary. Of particular interest is Jackson's Whydah *E. jacksoni*, the subject of an excellent and detailed study by V. D. van Someren (1958).

Pin-tailed Whydah *Vidua macroura*
The striated, sparrow-like female is only 4½ inches long, but the male in breeding plumage is nearly 13 inches, the difference being made up by the four, equal-length black and elongated central tail feathers. The bill in both sexes is pink and the male's plumage is conspicuously black-and-white. The male usually seems aggressive, particularly so during the breeding season when it is so readily recognized in its nuptial dress.

The Pin-tailed Whydah is polygamous and parasitic, it being said that the hosts are more than one species of waxbills, an unusual feature of the *Vidua*. It travels in large flocks, the male greatly outnumbered by females and immature birds, and roosts in company. The courtship flight is characteristic, the male hovering over the female sitting below.

Its diet consists mainly of grass and other seeds and it inhabits open grasslands, scrub and cultivated areas, including gardens. This is the most common species in Africa.

Golden Weaver *Ploceus subaureus*
This bird is easily confused with the Golden Palm Weaver *P. bojeri*, having very similar habits. The male, 6 inches long, is entirely yellow with a saffron head, the female is yellowish-olive and both sexes have reddish-pink eyes.

It is highly gregarious and there is some evidence that it is polygamous. It forms noisy, chattering, breeding-colonies in trees, bushes or reeds. The neat, strong nest, built almost entirely by the male, is well-woven with an entrance at the bottom, and is usually attached to a stalk by a single support.

Holub's Golden Weaver *Ploceus xanthops*
This is a large (8 inches), thickset weaver greenish-gold in colour, with an orange tinge on the upper breast and throat. The female is very similar, though paler. It is usually found in pairs, rarely in small parties, and is not gregarious.

The nest is a large one, rough and loosely woven of coarse grass and lined with finer grass. The male seems to build a number of nests, anything up to six, but only one of them is occupied. It is found in a variety of country, but shows a preference for swamps and marshes.

Red-naped Widow-bird *Euplectes ardens*
In some parts of its distribution the male widow-bird has only a crescent-shaped patch on the upper breast, yellow, orange or scarlet in colour, the rest of the plumage being black; but in other areas the crown and the neck are also scarlet. It is 11 inches long. The female is about 5 inches, much less colourful and difficult to tell from females of allied species, as is the male in non-breeding dress.

It is locally resident and partially migrant in East Africa, commonly found in small flocks in patches of grass in suitable country. The woven nest is usually slung in grass, lined with dry grass, and may have a porch.

White-headed Buffalo Weaver *Dinemellia dinemelli*
This is a large, dusky brown and white weaver belonging to the sub-family Bubalornithinae, about 9 inches long and having a reddish-orange rump, which is very conspicuous in flight. It seems to have no association with the buffalo in spite of its name. It will eat seed, fruit and insects and can be seen foraging for food, singly, in pairs or small parties on the ground in association with certain starlings.

The nest, often hung from the branch of a thorn tree, is an untidy, retort-like structure, with an entrance from below, made up of thorny twigs (and thus highly protective) and lined with grass or feathers. A conspicuous bird of dry thorn-bush country, it is very easily recognized in flight.

Left top to bottom The Vitelline Masked Weaver *Ploceus velatus* brings a piece of grass to its onion-shaped nest, and begins to weave it in.
Below and bottom A Grosbeak Weaver's nest at an early stage of its construction, showing how it is anchored on two upright reed stems.
Far left and centre The weaver continues to add material until the nest is complete.

37 Starlings

Members of the starling family (Sturnidae), numbering over a hundred, all belong to the Old World, though the Common Starling *Sturnus vulgaris* has been unwisely introduced in other parts of the world including America, with considerable breeding success. In East Africa, the family is represented by thirty-two species, three of which are endemic, and they are found in all types of wooded country. Perhaps the most common bird in Europe, it lives in close proximity to human habitation. With its familiar glossy black and more or less

speckled plumage, it offers a startling contrast to the colourful starlings of Africa.

Starlings are sturdy birds, varying in length from 7 to 17 inches, with strong legs and bills and a rapid and powerful flight. Although many of the species in the tropics are mainly arboreal, they are also at home on the ground, and can be seen actively running about foraging for food, which consists mainly of insects. However, they can be regarded as almost omnivorous as they are also partial to small fruits and seeds.

Many species are noisy, conspicuous and gregarious, some even during the breeding season, nesting in colonies. Most of them nest in holes in trees and rocks, some build weaver-like nests and quite a few have adapted to living in close association with human beings, taking advantage of artificial nesting sites such as crannies around buildings, in roofs under tiles, nest-boxes etc. A number of species, particularly those living in temperate areas, migrate in part during the winter, sometimes assembling in enormous numbers.

The family of starlings is divided into two sub-families, the true starlings (Sturninae) and the oxpeckers (Buphaginae). In East Africa, the former consists of thirty species divided amongst nine genera and the latter is made up of only two species of the single genus *Buphagus*. The majority of true starlings are beautiful, some startlingly so, and are loosely termed glossy starlings, although some authorities use this term in a restricted sense, only for members of the genus *Lamprotornis*.

Glossy starlings possess brilliantly coloured plumage, predominantly blue, green or purple with a metallic gloss, and are almost exclusively confined to Africa, where they are widespread. They are best viewed in bright sunlight when the iridescent colours are seen in all their glory. Pride of place among them all must go to the Golden-breasted Starling *Spreo regius*, 14 inches long, with its slim, long tail, metallic green and blue head, neck and upper parts. The upper breast is coloured violet and lower parts golden yellow.

Also spectacular is the Violet-backed Starling *Cinnyricinclus leucogaster*. The male has metallic violet-blue above, in some lights appearing plum-coloured or even crimson, and white underparts. Rare for the starlings, the female is quite different and almost dull. An abundant species found in the highlands and the lowlands, in open park-like country and in woodlands, is the Blue-eared Glossy Starling *Lamprotornis chalybaeus*, a metallic green bird, bluish in colour in certain lights, which has a wide distribution.

A few species of the true starlings are more homely looking. The Wattled Starling *Creatophora cinerea*, as its name suggests, develops a number of wattles on its head and neck during the breeding season. At this time, because they live together in large flocks, these starlings need a large supply of food. They look for vast concentrations of migratory flocks of locusts, then nest communally in nearby trees, feeding on the immature hoppers.

The two species of oxpeckers, perhaps more correctly known as tick-birds because of their feeding behaviour, are confined entirely to the Ethiopian Region. They overlap considerably where their ranges meet, the two species sometimes being observed on one animal. Although oxpeckers, because of their special feeding adaptation, differ from true starlings in having laterally flattened bills, very sharp, curved claws and a stiffened, long tail, there is little argument that they are aberrant members of the starling family.

Both species obtain their entire food supply from the hides of animals, both wild and domestic, preference being given to the larger mammals, but a well infested smaller 'host' is not ignored. Rhinoceros, giraffe, zebra, buffalo, various antelope, even wart-hog, and most domestic, preference being given to the larger mammals, although an infested smaller 'host' is not ignored. Rhinoceros, giraffe, zebra, buffalo, various antelope, even wart-hog, and most domestic stock, are visited in flocks by these birds and they are happily tolerated except by the elephant. The birds walk about on the animal in the manner of woodpeckers, their structural peculiarities, especially the stiffened tail and the sharp, curved claws, enabling them to maintain their hold and move about in any direction on the animal without difficulty. Their main nourishment comes from the engorged ticks, but flies, scar tissue, blood and living tissue, and discharge from open wounds on the 'hosts' are also taken.

As a consequence, the wound does not get a chance to heal and may even be enlarged. This has led to considerable argument as to whether tick-birds are beneficial or not. One school welcomes the attention to stock and the consequential cleansing of parasites, but the opposition believes that blood parasites may be transmitted by the birds, in addition to the damage caused to the hide.

Superb Starling *Spreo superbus*

This is a plump, short-tailed glossy starling about 7 inches long. It is readily recognized with its metallic greenish-blue back, black head and a narrow white band across the breast separating the metallic blue throat and breast from the bright chestnut belly. It occurs in thornbush and acacia country, and commonly seen feeding on the ground in small parties. The nest consists of a ball of grass with a tunnel entrance at the side, surrounded by thorny twigs; but it is also known to nest in holes in trees or cliffs or old nests of other birds. Normally four eggs are laid, which are incubated and brooded by both sexes.

Below, A red-billed Oxpecker *Buphagus erythrorhynchus* on its 'host', a Reticulated Giraffe. Their special, curved claws enable them to move in any direction on the host, without falling off.
Left, Plate 72 True to its name, the Superb Starling *Spreo superbus* has splendid, colourful plumage.

Notes on Colour Plates

It was originally my intention to include in the book a chapter or two on the technique of bird photography but basically this is universal, and there are a number of excellent books on the subject. Two recent publications, which can be read with profit are:

Hosking, E. and Gooders, J. (1973) *Wildlife Photography,* London: Hutchinson & Co. (Publishers) Ltd.

Turner Ettlinger, D.M. ed. (1974) *Natural History Photography*, London: Academic Press.

However, it is hardly ever possible to photograph a bird according to the 'book' and so I have written, at length where necessary, about how, when and where the illustrations were taken and in what way the standard technique was adapted to meet a particular problem. But first, a brief note about the equipment and the films used. All the photographs in this book were taken with a Leicaflex SL or the Leica M3 with a Visoflex housing. Both were usually fitted with some kind of a rapid-focussing device and used with a variety of lenses, varying in focal length from 135mm to 560mm, but mostly with the Telyt f4.8 280mm lens. All the colour plates were made from 35mm Kodachrome–X transparencies. I prefer this film to slower ones, because the extra speed (ASA 64) allows me to use a faster shutter speed and because results with slower films tend to be 'larger than life'. The black and white photographs were taken on Kodak Plus–X film (ASA 125) and developed by the 1+3 dilution method in Kodak Microdol–X developer.

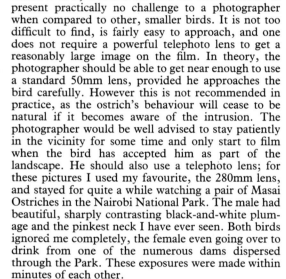

Plates 2 & 3, Ostrich. At first the ostrich seems to present practically no challenge to a photographer when compared to other, smaller birds. It is not too difficult to find, is fairly easy to approach, and one does not require a powerful telephoto lens to get a reasonably large image on the film. In theory, the photographer should be able to get near enough to use a standard 50mm lens, provided he approaches the bird carefully. However this is not recommended in practice, as the ostrich's behaviour will cease to be natural if it becomes aware of the intrusion. The photographer would be well advised to stay patiently in the vicinity for some time and only start to film when the bird has accepted him as part of the landscape. He should also use a telephoto lens; for these pictures I used my favourite, the 280mm lens, and stayed for quite a while watching a pair of Masai Ostriches in the Nairobi National Park. The male had beautiful, sharply contrasting black-and-white plumage and the pinkest neck I have ever seen. Both birds ignored me completely, the female even going over to drink from one of the numerous dams dispersed through the Park. These exposures were made within minutes of each other.

Plate 4, White Pelicans. Lake Nakuru, since the successful introduction of the fish *Tilapia grahami* in 1961, has supported a large population of fish-eating birds, White Pelicans being predominant. At certain times of the day they congregate in vast numbers at the mouth of the rivers which feed the lake, and drink and bathe in the fresh water. The Nderit River runs into the south-east corner of the lake and one afternoon, when the light was in the right direction, it was possible to discern a flight path of the pelicans flying between the lake and a pool upstream. I decided to try some flight shots with the 550mm lens, as it was impossible to get close enough to use a smaller one. Normally, for flight shots, which are always difficult anyway, I hand-hold the 280mm lens so as to be able to follow the subject while trying to keep it constantly in focus, a very tricky manoeuvre which inevitably results in a large number of wasted shots. The 560mm lens is too heavy to hold steadily in the hand, so it was clamped on to a bracket on the car door. The shutter was set at 1/1000 second, the lens pointed and focussed on a spot in the sky, hopefully worked out from the flight path, and the result shown here was the only really successful shot of the afternoon. I was particularly pleased with the background which shows the magnificent forest on the hill, a unique feature of Lake Nakuru National Park.

Plate 5, Pink-backed Pelicans. Perhaps the most difficult aspect of against-the-light photography is deciding what exposure to use. There is no 'correct' exposure because a colour film cannot cope satisfactorily with a subject which has a wide range of contrast. Something has to be sacrificed: one can expose for the highlight or the shadow. For the highlight, the main subject may come out as a silhouette; over-exposure, on the other hand, will burn out the highlights and also most of the colour from the whole picture. The solution is to 'bracket', which means making a series of exposures grouped round the estimated average exposure. This is what I did in the present case. The pelicans were gliding gently backwards and forwards, allowing a number of shots to be made, and this exposure was the one finally selected as it conveyed the exact quality of luminosity and glitter which had first attracted my attention to the subject.

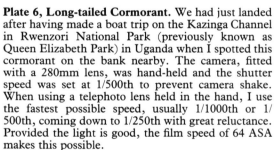

Plate 6, Long-tailed Cormorant. We had just landed after having made a boat trip on the Kazinga Channel in Rwenzori National Park (previously known as Queen Elizabeth Park) in Uganda when I spotted this cormorant on the bank nearby. The camera, fitted with a 280mm lens, was hand-held and the shutter speed was set at 1/500th to prevent camera shake. When using a telephoto lens held in the hand, I use the fastest possible speed, usually 1/1000th or 1/500th, coming down to 1/250th with great reluctance. Provided the light is good, the film speed of 64 ASA makes this possible.

Plate 7, White-necked Cormorants. Even if your main interest is not bird photography, I can think of nothing more satisfying than an early morning boat trip on Lake Naivasha. These White-necked Cormorants, drying their wings on a small island before plunging back into the lake in search of more prey or flying off to new feeding areas, were photographed with the 280mm lens. A shoulder-grip and a motor were used and as we drifted gently towards the island I made a series of exposures at 1/500th second, sitting on the bow of the boat. The result conveys to me the very essence of the freshness of an early morning on Lake Naivasha.

Plate 8, Darter. This is another shot taken at Lake Naivasha, again from a boat, but this time not on such a brilliant day. The darter was drying its wings on a floating log and the almost monochromatic effect of the grey sky and water on the dull plumage is particularly pleasing to me. Once more the camera with the 280mm lens was hand-held and the shutter speed was 1/250th second. Darters spend much of their time perched like this, with their wings spread.

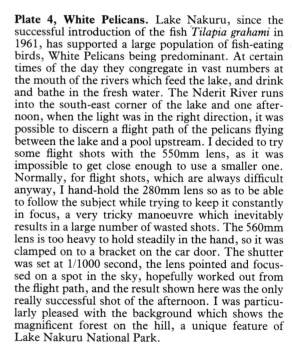

Plate 9, Goliath Heron. Yet another shot taken at Lake Naivasha, also from a boat. A hand-held camera with the 280mm lens, set at 1/500th second, and a slow quiet approach was all that was necessary to capture this, the largest of all the herons. This handsome bird, portrayed against the lush green background, is my favourite of many pictures taken of this heron.

Plate 10, Squacco Heron. Perhaps this is an appropriate time to mention the use of a car as a mobile hide or blind. A great deal of one's photography in Africa is done in National Parks. With very few exceptions, the visitor is not allowed to leave his car while in the park, other than at the lodge, and must therefore make his exposures from inside the vehicle. This is not such a disadvantage as it may seem. The mammals and birds in the parks are used to cars and do not associate them with any danger, and so remain undisturbed. The photographer by himself, or with an equally keen companion, is obviously better off than one in a crowded bus. A four-wheel-drive vehicle is ideal, because it allows one to get to places inaccessible to ordinary cars and its higher viewpoint is often an advantage. I use such a vehicle all the time. Provided the occupant is prepared to sit still and not make any sudden movements, he rarely needs to hide behind a canvas screen. The car is driven slowly to a suitable site, such as a lake shore; immediately a number of birds will move or fly away. This is where patience is essential. They may return in a few minutes, a few hours or not at all! So a long, and sometimes fruitless, wait is necessary. Reading a book may help to pass the time but I tend to read the same paragraph over and over again. Alternatively, just as I have got my nose in the book, an interesting bird comes into view and promptly flies away before I can put the book down! So one has to be on the alert the whole time. The camera with its telephoto lens can be rested on a small sandbag or a beanbag, which in turn rests on the car door. This holds the camera quite steady and prevents shake, but of course the car engine must be switched off to avoid vibrations. Because of the amount of time I spend in the car, I have an ingenious clamp fitted onto the door, which I can raise, lower, tilt or level and the camera can be left firmly fixed onto this. All this preamble to tell you that the Squacco Heron was shot with the 560mm lens from my 'mobile hide'.

Plate 11, Cattle Egret. On checking my note-books, I was amazed to find that this photograph was taken more than twelve years ago. I recall that Kodachrome–X film had just been introduced in this country and this was one of the earliest shots I took with it. Cattle Egrets are not particularly photogenic at any time, but I was agreeably surprised to find how well the new film had coped with the high contrast of a white bird taken almost against the light. With its soft gradations, it was just the type of fast film I had been looking for and I have used it ever since. The egret was pictured at Amboseli when it was a Game Reserve, now changed to a National Park. Broadly speaking, a Game Reserve is an area where wildlife is protected but where human beings can continue to live. Inevitably there is competition, particularly for water. The Masai, especially during the dry season, used to take their vast herds of domestic cattle to water and feed in the very heart of Amboseli where permanent fresh water is always available. The wild animals suffered as a result and the eventual solution was to establish the area as a National Park where the rights of game are sacrosant and human beings are considered to be intruders.

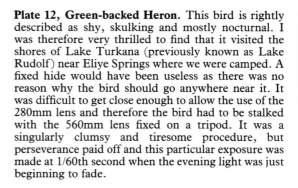

Plate 12, Green-backed Heron. This bird is rightly described as shy, skulking and mostly nocturnal. I was therefore very thrilled to find that it visited the shores of Lake Turkana (previously known as Lake Rudolf) near Eliye Springs where we were camped. A fixed hide would have been useless as there was no reason why the bird should go anywhere near it. It was difficult to get close enough to allow the use of the 280mm lens and therefore the bird had to be stalked with the 560mm lens fixed on a tripod. It was a singularly clumsy and tiresome procedure, but perseverance paid off and this particular exposure was made at 1/60th second when the evening light was just beginning to fade.

Plate 13, Black-headed Heron. Those who live in Nairobi are fortunate to have a National Park on their doorstep, only a few minutes drive from the centre of the city. The plains, riverine forests, woodlands and scrub provide a variety of habitats, and birdlife abounds. A number of artificial dams have been created and I have spent many happy hours sitting in the car on the edge of a dam watching and waiting for things to happen. Black-headed Herons are common enough, seen almost as frequently in grassland looking for insects, as near water. I was driving out of the Park, after the usual pleasurable morning, when I came across this bird in the reeds near the largest dam. Bigger birds do not seem to mind cars and the 280mm lens was all that was necessary to get a picture of the heron in particularly attractive surroundings.

Plate 14, Yellow-billed Stork. There was to be a total eclipse of the sun on the 30 June 1973 and one of the best places from which to view it was Loiyangalani, situated on the east shore and almost at the southern end of Lake Turkana. Scientists from all over the world were going there and the East African Natural History Society and the National Museum sent a team to study the behaviour of birds and mammals before, during and after the eclipse. I decided to go too. My main intention was to photograph the various stages of the eclipse, but while waiting for D-day I spent my time driving along the lake shore looking for birds to photograph. Great care had to be exercised as the shore was very treacherous. The surface looked hard and perfectly safe to drive on and in some places this was so, but in others it was very deceptive. One could break through the top crust and get bogged in the glutinous mud underneath. I had been warned and so drove carefully, having to extricate my front wheels only twice by putting the vehicle into four-wheel-drive and reversing; but a friend managed to break through with all four wheels and it took two days to dig him out. I photographed many unfamiliar birds, but strangely enough it was at Lake Turkana that I took my best picture of the Yellow-billed Stork, which is common everywhere there is water.

Plate 15, Saddle-billed Stork. A pair of Saddle-billed Storks were discovered within sight of our camp on the first evening we arrived at Lake Jipe. I knew the direction of the light would be just right in the morning, and so set up a standard hide on the edge of the open patch of water. I went into the hide the next morning, but the light was variable, with the sun going in and out of clouds. The birds were busy feeding, on the move all the time and it was difficult, if not impossible, to keep them in focus and maintain the correct exposure. However, I did the best I could under the circumstances and made a number of exposures until the light moved too far overhead. This is one of them. The following morning was brilliantly

sunny. I was having an early breakfast in camp, anxious to get into my hide, and make the most of the favourable light conditions, when suddenly my wife noticed the pair of storks take off and fly right across to the other side of the lake. They had stayed quite happily in the pool for two days and then, for no apparent reason, they left. There is a moral in this story for bird photographers: birds are unpredictable and so is the weather. Conditions are hardly ever perfect and it is important to take what pictures you can when the opportunity first arises, otherwise the chance may be lost for ever. They may turn out to be only recording shots, but you can always hope that things will be better the next day. I must confess that I often fail to take my own advice.

Plate 16, Sacred Ibis. As I have said earlier, flight shots are far from easy but it is a very good trick to slowly approach a bird sitting on a tree, with a hand-held camera (preferably fitted with a shoulder grip) set at 1/500th or 1/1000th second. Keeping the subject continuously in focus, approach until the bird thinks you are too close for comfort and takes off. At this moment, if you are alert *and* lucky, your shutter will go off and you should get your picture. This Sacred Ibis was sitting on the top of a tall dead tree and I was in a slowly-drifting boat.

Plate 18 and 17, Sacred Ibises, Glossy Ibis. Once again we were at Lake Jipe and as we sat in camp with a drink, watching the sun setting in a riot of colour behind the North Para Mountains of Tanzania, we saw flight upon flight of birds travelling from south to north, from their feeding grounds to their roosts. Since then, every time I have spent an evening on the shore of the lake, I have had my camera at the ready. The technique is not difficult. The shutter is set at 1/500th second and the camera is fitted with the 280mm lens and a motor drive. Having taken the meter reading from the sky like all exposures for sunset shots, all you need is a friend with keen eyesight to warn you of the birds' approach; a ready trigger finger and the good luck that the birds will fly through the point in the sky on which you have focussed. Needless to say, sometimes the birds do not come at all or are hopelessly close, and at other times the sun disappears behind a large dark cloud just at that moment. However, I have had a lot of fun trying and a little success too. The Glossy Ibis, standing at the edge of the same lake, was shot with the 280mm lens clamped to the car door.

Plate 19, Hadada Ibis. At least two, and sometimes three or four Hadada Ibis seem to live in the valley at the bottom of our garden, though I have never discovered where they roost or nest. They can often be seen walking about in the garden looking for insects. And they can certainly be heard! Their raucous calls often wake us in the morning and sometimes even during a bright moonlit night. I have often stalked them with a camera but without much success as they appear drab brown on the photograph, unless you catch them in the right light. I was sitting in a hide on the bank of an artificial dam on a coffee farm managed by a friend. The dam was full of fish and therefore a favourite haunt of the Pied Kingfisher, which was my reason for being there. I noticed a pair of Hadada Ibis appear on the 'blind' side of the hide and, after watching them briefly, gave up all thought of photographing them. Suddenly, one bird flew up and occupied the perch normally favoured by the kingfishers. The light was just right and the exposure was made with the 280mm lens.

Plates 20 & 22, Greater Flamingos, Greater Flamingo. Both these exposures were made at Lake Elmenteita in the Kenya Rift Valley in 1966. Greater Flamingo have successfully nested there infrequently in the past and not at all for some years now, their favourite nesting sites being taken over by the larger and clumsier White Pelicans. I therefore consider myself very fortunate to have had the opportunity of photographing them then. Lake Elmenteita is a shallow, alkaline lake, the depth nowhere exceeding about five feet. The flamingos nest on a number of lava outcrops which form small islands in the lake. The question was how to approach them without causing them to desert, a very real risk in view of their timidity, particularly during nesting time. A floating hide was the obvious answer, but there were two problems: one was how to propel it, and the second was how to dislodge it if its floating drums got snagged on underwater rocks. The eventual solution was to make a hole in the centre of the floating platform on which the hide was built. The photographer, in the hide, put his legs and body through the hole and walked in the water along the bottom of the lake, pushing and manoeuvering the hide, having securely tied all his equipment safely out of the way on its framework. Immersion in alkaline water for any length of time is not a pleasant experience, but luckily there had been good rains recently and alkalinity of the water was not so concentrated. Provided I moved very slowly, the birds did not object to the approach of the floating hide and it was possible to get quite close to the islands. It was a fantastic experience to get so near to the breeding colony and one I shall never forget. The single female with young was taken with the 200mm lens and the shot of the group, showing territorial threat display, was made with the 135mm lens. In each case, I underexposed deliberately by one whole stop to keep details of the white feathers, which otherwise would have burnt out.

Plate 21, Lesser Flamingo. Central Island in Lake Turkana is an extinct volcano, partially immersed in the lake. It has three crater lakes, of which Crater Lake B attracts the most interesting birdlife. Flocks of Lesser Flamingo are often observed in it varying in number from 10,000 to 50,000. On my second visit to the island I camped with some friends for a couple of nights on the shore of the lake and worked in the crater during the daytime. We set up two standard hides, having manhandled them up the precipitous slope and down the crater wall, a debilitating experience, due to the fierce sun and high humidity. The afternoon sun lit up the opposite wall, its yellow reflection in the blue water turning it to different shades of green. The disturbed flamingos soon returned as the hides were put up very quickly. I spent the first afternoon photographing the birds and their ever-changing reflections in the water. During my stay in the hide, I had observed that the flamingos crossed and re-crossed the lake fairly frequently, so I decided to try to get photographs of individual birds in flight against the water. The next day, I sat higher up the crater, with the hand-held camera fitted with the 280mm lens and motor, and used up a lot of film trying to get the kind of pictures I had visualized. This photograph, shot at 1/1000th second was one of the very few successes of that afternoon. However, our excitement was not over yet. That night a tremendous storm blew up with gale-force winds and torrential rain, accompanied by continuous peals of thunder and flashes of lightning. All three tents were blown down, one of them being torn in half, and only the weight of our bodies and in my case, the weight of the camera equipment, prevented them blowing away into the nearby lake to join a heavy table which had

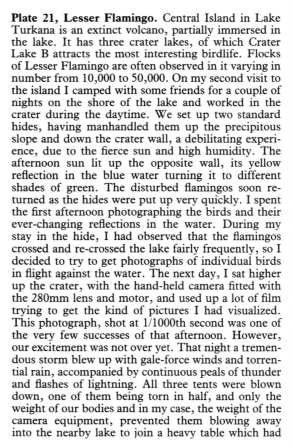

travelled over 150 feet. We lay soaking wet in our flattened tents until daylight, when we staggered out to survey the wreckage. It was really quite frightening at the time, but now looked back upon as rather an adventure!

Plates 23 and 1 (Frontispiece). Fulvous Tree Ducks, White-faced Tree Ducks. Lake Jipe in the Tsavo West National Park, where these two pictures were taken, is a favourite haunt for large numbers of ducks. When making these photographs, I was using the 280mm lens fitted on the door clamp of the car and spent many happy hours sitting quietly or driving along the shore of the lake in search of a subject.

Plates 24 and 25 Egyptian Geese, Spur-winged Geese. These two photographs were also taken from the car, parked beside the lake. Once the subjects had appeared, I stayed with them, making a number of exposures. It is a mistake to economize on film: the opportunity for a particular shot may never come again, and if you rely on only one or two shots, it is disappointing later to discover that the bird has blinked or moved its head at the moment of exposure!

Plate 26, Knob-billed Goose. We were told that cormorants and darters were nesting on a small island in Lake Naivasha and that it was a sight well worth seeing, not that we needed much persuasion. We went to the Lake Hotel, which is situated on the shore and hired a boat and boatman, who was very co-operative and knowledgeable about the problem of photographing lake birds. The Knob-billed Goose was photographed from the boat during this visit. The level of the lake has fluctuated considerably over the years and the goose is perched on an old fence post which is almost totally immersed. Water-lilies grow profusely on the lake, very attractive to see and to photograph, besides providing a suitable habitat for coots and lily-trotters, but somewhat of a nuisance to boat propellers.

Plate 27, Ruppell's Griffon and White-backed Vultures. Because of their feeding habits, vultures are regarded as unclean by most people. Just to prove them wrong, a number of species took to visiting two adjacent dams in the Nairobi National Park in the latter part of 1973, where they bathed and cleaned themselves thoroughly before spreading out their wings to dry in the sun. It was possible to see four or five species of vulture at any one time, numbering up to a hundred birds. From a photographic point of view they posed a problem. They were easy enough to

approach in a car, but it was almost midday before they started to congregate, flying in one by one, sometimes joined by a few Marabou Storks. Of course, by this time the light was practically overhead. In temperate zones it is possible to make exposures during most of the day, but in the tropics it is advisable to confine any photography to before 11 a.m. at the latest, and after 3 p.m. at the earliest. Otherwise the deep, dense shadows make exposures very tricky and give unsatisfactory results. Fortunately in this case the ground was reflecting some light back onto the birds, but even then I bracketed my exposures carefully by half stops and managed to produce this one acceptable picture among several taken. I was particularly pleased to get these two vultures side by side, the Ruppell's Griffon on the left and the White-backed on the right, as I often find them difficult to identify apart.

Plate 28, Pale Chanting Goshawk. I have never found raptors easy to photograph. They generally perch on tall trees, and aiming the camera from a low viewpoint is far from satisfactory. The best pictures are taken from platform hides built to bring the birds to eye-level, but this is only possible at their nests. I was particularly fortunate in finding this goshawk perched on a rock in the Samburu Game Reserve about 200 miles north of Nairobi. It is a place well worth visiting to see Reticulated Giraffe, Grevy's Zebra, Gerenuk, the Somali Ostrich, and other birds not readily seen elsewhere. Critical focussing, with the 560mm lens at full aperture was necessary to separate the bird from the otherwise intrusive branches in the foreground.

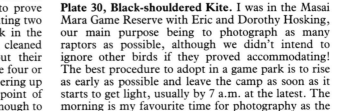

Plate 29, African Fish Eagle. To those of us who live in Africa, the call of the fish eagle is more evocative than any other bird call. To be awakened in the early morning, near a lake shore, by the sound of a pair of these birds calling is an unforgettable and haunting experience. The palaeontologists Richard and Meave Leakey spend as much time as they possibly can in the wild, desert country on the eastern shore of Lake Turkana, working on prehistoric sites in the area. A pair of African Fish Eagles were often seen in the vicinity but there was no tree in that barren area on which the birds could perch and call, as they normally do. So the Leakeys dragged a dead tree back from the interior, and placed it on the foreshore of the lake. The birds were soon perching and they and the Leakeys were happy. We visited Koobi Fora in October 1975 and I decided to photograph the fish eagles on their dead tree, which had such an attractive shape. There was no time to put up a hide, so stalking them was the only answer. I used the 280mm lens and stopped every few yards to make a couple of exposures. The pair of birds let me get reasonably close, neither of them flying away until I had got some satisfying shots. When one flew off I knew that the second would follow pretty soon, and so kept it continuously in focus while getting closer and closer. It eventually took off, and I just managed to make this one exposure at 1/1000th second.

Plate 30, Black-shouldered Kite. I was in the Masai Mara Game Reserve with Eric and Dorothy Hosking, our main purpose being to photograph as many raptors as possible, although we didn't intend to ignore other birds if they proved accommodating! The best procedure to adopt in a game park is to rise as early as possible and leave the camp as soon as it starts to get light, usually by 7 a.m. at the latest. The morning is my favourite time for photography as the light continues to improve during the day; in the evening just as one has been lucky enough to get close to a bird after a long and arduous stalk, the sun decides to set. So the drill is to go out early, return at midday for a brief rest and set out again by 4 p.m. to make the most of the remaining couple of hours or so of daylight. In any case, bird activity is at a minimum during the heat of the middle of the day. We had only just left camp when Dorothy spotted this kite sitting on top of a medium-sized tree, well off the road. Cameras were put on clamps, sandbags made ready, and we moved very slowly in four-wheel-drive across the rough terrain, to approach the bird from the right direction for the light. We adopted the usual procedure of taking photographs at intervals as we got closer and closer; this is one of my last exposures with the 560mm lens before the kite decided that it had co-operated for long enough, and flew away.

Plate 31, Helmeted Guineafowl. You see these birds quite frequently in small flocks, and it is easy to focus on the white spots on a black background (I maintain that Zebras were also designed to help photographers); but they are certainly not easy to photograph satisfactorily. They are busy creatures, continuously on the move and so going in and out of focus all the time. I spent nearly two hours one morning with this particular bird, and ended up with a large number of wasted exposures to show for it. This one was taken at the split second when something had distracted the guineafowl from its constant feeding activity. The 560mm lens at f5.6 has isolated the bird from its background which, if it too had been sharp, would have distracted the eye.

Plate 32, Yellow-necked Spurfowl. These are normally ground birds and so inevitably one has to shoot down on them from a car, not an ideal angle for the camera, as the body hides the spurs on their legs. Therefore this exposure appeals to me, not only because the bird is at eye level, but because the rugged tree forms a pleasant contrast to the bird and the lush green background. The spurfowl is reasonably common everywhere, some even seem to have taken up residence in the wild part of our Nairobi garden for the past few months, but this photograph was taken at Amboseli.

Plate 33, Crowned Crane. In the days before Lake Naivasha had become the big tourist attraction it is today, it was my practice to set up a bird hide on the shore on a Saturday afternoon, go into it early on Sunday morning, with something to eat and drink, and be prepared to spend the whole day there. It was a 'wait-and-see' exercise. Sometimes nothing happened from a photographic point of view, and at other times, it did. On this particular morning a pair of Crowned Cranes decided to visit me and this is one of the photographs I took with the 280mm lens.

Plate 34, Crowned Plover. I was making one of my fairly regular visits to the Nairobi National Park one morning, and took a well-used track to my favourite dam. Driving very slowly as I invariably do, I was suddenly startled by an angry alarm call. I jammed on my brakes and looked out to find an irate Crowned Plover standing over its nest, hardly twelve inches from the front wheel of the car, but fortunately just off the track. I backed out carefully, but I suspect that the nest may well have come to a sad end later because of its situation. When the bird sat tight, it was impossible to distinguish it from the surrounding

stones; it was almost perfect camouflaged. This was another bird, photographed in the same vicinity, where it seemed to be interested in a nesting site very similar to the one mentioned above, but fortunately away from the track.

Plate 35, Blacksmith Plover. These plovers can hardly be described as 'photographers' friends'. In fact, they can be very irritating when one is carefully stalking a bird or trying to set up a hide quietly and quickly. They fly repeatedly at the intruder, making their characteristic clinking call and warning every bird within miles, or so it seems to the irate photographer. On the other hand they will sit very tight when at the nest. I recall one plover sitting on its nest made amidst buffalo droppings, letting me get almost to within touching distance without making a sound. The subject of this photograph allowed a very close approach so that the image practically filled the frame with the 280mm lens. Notice that the bird is not incubating the egg in the traditional way by sitting on it, but rather crouching over it, partially to shade it and partially to leave an airspace over it to prevent overheating. The bird's open beak is also a mechanism for losing body heat. Unless the light is just right, it is almost impossible to get the dark-red eye differentiated from the black head.

Plate 36, Three-banded Plover. A nondescript plover at first glance, this bird is frequently found in mudflats on lake shores or river banks. On closer scrutiny however, the red eye-ring and red beak with a black tip make it a handsome bird. This photograph demonstrates a very important part of my technique; I should like to emphasize that I take great pains to isolate the subject from the background. This has an almost three-dimensional effect, the only sharp part of the picture being the bird and especially its eye. Technically this is achieved by using as wide an aperture as possible, thus getting a minimum depth of field, and a correspondingly faster shutter speed, which has the additional advantage of freezing any bird movement and minimizing camera shake. The 560mm lens has a maximum aperture of f5.6 and the 280mm lens of f4.8. I do not think it is necessary to have lenses of wider aperture than these, as they are much more expensive and, being bigger and heavier, difficult to manipulate.

Plate 37, Spurwing Plovers. These birds are highly territorial at breeding time, vigorously and vociferously defending their territory from any intruder, but at other times they are found in small flocks, generally on the edge of water looking for crustaceae and insects. I was intrigued by the pattern made by the movement of the plovers as they ran about on the shore of Lake Turkana, against a background of gently breaking waves. Through the lens, the almost monochromatic effect was appealing and this is one of a number of exposures I made that afternoon with the 280mm lens.

Plates 38 and 40. Curlew Sandpiper, Greenshank. Although mention has been made previously of Lake Turkana, this seems an appropriate place in which to describe it in more detail because of its ornithological interest. It is the largest alkaline lake in the world, with an area of 2470 square miles and lies in the Rift Valley in northern Kenya. Its northern end is just inside Ethiopia, from the highlands of which it gets its main supply of water via the Omo River. Known as the Jade Sea because of its bluish-green colour, it

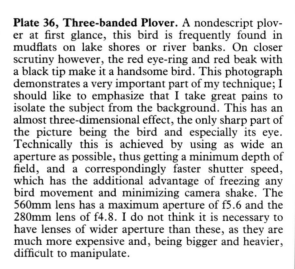

makes a startling contrast to the inhospitable, rugged lava desert which surrounds it. The lake is not easy to get to by road, but many fishermen fly there to catch the spectacular Nile Perch, and bird-lovers visit it, not only for the dry-country birds which abound in the area, but also for the large number of Palaearctic migrants which visit the lake during the European winter. Both these exposures were made in the Ferguson's Gulf area of the lake, working from a hide built on a sandbank in the middle of the gulf. My most vivid impression, besides the wonder of being surrounded by hundreds of skimmers and terns, was of almost unbearable heat. The lake is situated 1200 feet above sea level, and with the high humidity, hours spent in the hide were like being in a Turkish bath. There is a serious danger of dehydration and the visitor is strongly advised to replace the salt loss suffered during heavy and almost continuous perspiration.

Plate 39, Little Stint. This is a common winter visitor and was photographed at a very accessible alkaline lake, only sixty-five miles south-west of Nairobi. This is Lake Magadi, which was the scene of the famous rescue operation of the Lesser Flamingo in 1962. There are a number of hot springs in the area and this exposure was made near one of them, with the 560mm lens. I was attracted to it by the pattern and colour of the water and the rocks, which seemed to complement those of the bird.

Plate 41, Avocets. Ever since I read the fascinating account of their behaviour in V. D. van Someren's 'A Bird-watcher in Kenya', I had wanted to photograph Avocets, particularly at nesting time. Lake Magadi was the place to go as some breed there regularly every year, soon after the long rains in April. So I had visited Lake Magadi for many years, but time and again I had failed, either getting there too late or just not managing to find the correct site. But in 1975 my luck changed. I was told in May that the birds were nesting, but unfortunately could not get away at that particular time. However, accompanied by a friend, I went there in mid-June and was agreeably surprised to find nests and young at various stages of development. This particular exposure was made with the hand-held 280mm lens at 1/1000th second, at a shallow lagoon where there were three young chicks, hunting for food in the water. As I approached the adults they put on this diversionary display.

Plate 42, Black-winged Stilt. This is yet another example of how well Kodachrome–X manages to produce delicate tones under harsh light conditions. Even the pink of the legs is not aggressive and no details are lost in the white plumage. This is the kind of colour photography that appeals to me most. The exposure was made with the 280mm lens.

Plate 43, Water Dikkop. This shot was made at Lake Jipe using the 560mm lens and once again a full open aperture was used to give a very shallow depth of field, so that only the bird is in sharp focus. Note the large eye, typical of a nocturnal feeder.

Plate 44, Spotted Stone Curlews. Stone curlews confine their main activities to the hours of dusk and darkness, lying in deep shade during the daylight

hours. We had been driving rather haphazardly round the Samburu Game Reserve and were on our way back to camp in the evening, when these birds were spotted. I started making exposures from a distance, gradually driving closer and closer; but the stone curlews stayed put and eventually, as can be seen, practically filled the frame with the 280mm lens. The light was quite poor by this time and the successful exposure of 1/60th second would not have been possible without the door clamp holding the camera, although a sandbag would have served equally well as a support.

Plates 45 & 46, Two-banded Courser, Chestnut-bellied Sandgrouse. Both these exposures were made in the dry country area of Lake Magadi. Photographically they presented no particular problem, the difficulty being to find the birds! Even after the courser had been spotted, it was necessary to keep it continuously in view, otherwise it immediately 'disappeared' into the background. It seems to me that the method of differential focussing has been specially successful here as it separates the bird from its surroundings much more effectively than the human eye can do. The sandgrouse was so sure of its camouflage that it continued to sit tight on the nest even when approached quite closely; it would never have been discovered had it not been for the sharp and experienced eye of my friend, ornithologist Alec Forbes-Watson. We found two more nests in the vicinity by sheer chance, flushing the parent birds accidently when we approached.

Plate 47, Pink-breasted Dove. One of the easiest ways to photograph birds, particularly seed-eaters, is to attract them to a bird-table in your garden, but here is a word of warning about its placement. The table should be a clear three to four feet above ground, preferably on a single upright support; it should have a good area of visibility all round, and be placed not very far from a convenient bush. All this is to discourage cats or other predators from taking the feeding birds unawares. The next step is to provide a convenient perch near the bird-table, set up the hide, and then await your opportunity. This is an ideal way for beginners to start working from a hide and is how the dove was photographed. The branch was carefully selected for its photogenic quality and placed in relation to the hide and the table so that the latter was invisible from the camera's viewpoint; the lawn then made a perfect background.

Plate 48, Speckled Pigeons. This was another occasion when I sat in the hide on the mudflats of Lake Naivasha waiting for something to happen. It was during the limited duck-shooting season, when some hopeful hunter had put down grain to attract his unwary prey. No ducks came, but a lot of other birds did, including these pigeons. I took a number of shots of individual birds with the 280mm lens, but this is one of my favourites. Note the nicitating membrane covering the eye of the drinking bird.

Plate 49, Mackinder's Eagle-Owl. We had gone to spend Christmas on Island Camp in the middle of Lake Baringo, one of the chain of lakes on the floor of the Rift Valley in Kenya. I had known that there was a semi-tame Mackinder's Eagle-Owl there, far from its normal habitat, which had been reared from a fledgling. It must have been photographed innumerable times by visitors using a flash when as a young bird it would come to sit near the dining room banda

at night. However, it was my intention to photograph it by daylight, as I do not particularly like using a flash, though one has little alternative when photographing nocturnal birds. On this particular occasion, I made enquiries and was informed that the owl was now fully adult and no longer so confiding and tame, spent most of its daylight hours roosting in a tall tree and never visited the banda. Eventually I located the bird very high up in a tree amongst thickish foliage, fast asleep. I set up a tripod with the 560mm lens so that the subject nicely filled the frame, and waited for it to waken. After numerous visits during the late afternoon and early evening, when I had almost given up hope, the owl awoke. The light was poor by then, and needed an exposure of 1/15th second at full aperture. There was serious danger of subject movement as the owl peered down inquisitively at me, but I made a number of exposures, this being one of the few sharp ones. Note the difference in the size of the two irises: the one nearer the direction of the setting sun is smaller.

Plate 50, Pied Kingfisher. This picture was something of a bonus. I had set up the hide to try to photograph the Giant Kingfisher, which failed to come to the tree when the light was bright; however, the Pied Kingfisher did – and did so quite frequently. It would perch watchfully on a branch, suddenly take off to dive into the water, returning, successful or otherwise, to the same branch or one nearby. I was fascinated by the shape of these branches against the out-of-focus background and made numerous exposures, of which I find this the most pleasing. This bird is very photogenic, with its contrasting plumage.

Plate 51, Malachite Kingfisher. Although I had been using hides for some time, photographing this kingfisher was the first occasion when I really felt that I had mastered the technique. I not only gained confidence, but learnt an enormous amount from the experience. On one of our regular visits to Lake Naivasha, a series of brilliant flashes of colour drew our attention to a pair of Malachite Kingfishers digging their nest hole in a freshly dug bank near the lake shore. They were very busy and we left them to their task, returning some three weeks later. By this time, the eggs had been laid, incubated and hatched, as was obvious from the feeding activity of the parents. I quickly assembled a hide frame and moved it into the right position. Next I started putting together a second frame, the idea being to use it elsewhere on the lake shore, thus giving the birds time to get used to the first frame near their nest. To my surprise, within minutes, they were using it as a perch before going into the nest. Since the birds were so unperturbed, I put the canvas over the frame and entered the hide. They took no notice at all and I sat there absorbed, making the occasional exposure and marvelling at the wonder of sitting only a few feet away from these enchanting birds, which were completely unconcerned by my presence. It was only after I had taken a number of exposures that I realized that the perch they were using had a very fussy background of weeds which would conflict with the beautiful lines and colours of the kingfishers. So the next day I changed my viewpoint, provided a more attractive perch, and this is one of the shots I took using the plain bank as a background. I have photographed the Malachite Kingfisher many times since, but never again with the same degree of pleasure and satisfaction. I must add that I have never received quite the same degree of co-operation from any other bird. One of this pair would even perch, once in a while, on the end of the lens projecting from the hide canvas!

Plate 52, Giant Kingfisher. It is not often that one has an opportunity to get a good view of a Giant Kingfisher, let alone photograph it. One day, in the magazine 'Africana' I saw a series of fascinating photographs taken by Frants Hartmann showing sequences of this kingfisher catching, breaking up and then eating fish. Being a generous friend, Frants readily agreed to my request to visit his farm about twenty miles out of Nairobi and use his set-up to photograph the kingfishers fishing in the artificial dam. It necessitated an early start to get to the farm and into the hide by daybreak. The birds were active soon after dawn, when the light was not really bright enough to get good action photographs, especially as the sun took some time to clear the small hill behind the hide. Nevertheless I spent four happy mornings there and was amazed to discover the size of fish these kingfishers caught. No wonder they were satiated after one or two such catches and could not be bothered to hunt any more later in the day, when for me the light became better. This was one of the few good shots I got, taken with a 400mm lens which I rarely use. The positions of the hide and the perch being fixed, I could only control the image size by using different focal length lenses. I intended to go there again, but alas, the long rains came, the water of the dam became turgid, fish couldn't be seen and the pair of Giant Kingfishers left. They have not been back since but, hopefully, one day they will return and so shall I.

Plate 53, Carmine Bee-eater. These bee-eaters were nesting in a colony, of about 200 holes dug in flat ground in dry, sandy bush country, not far from Lake Turkana. Some friends were urging me to photograph the bee-eaters, but a trip to that area is not so readily arranged and it was some weeks before I could go. By this time the breeding was drawing to a close and feeding activity was at a minimum. It was very difficult, if not impossible, to tell which nests were still functioning and although I set up my hide near them, I had no luck. Fortunately the birds were using a tree nearby as a perch, where they frequently sat, prey in beak, before flying to the nest and this is where the exposure was made. What surprised me was the birds' lack of urgency, as they quite often sat on the branch with the insect for minutes on end before flying in to feed their young.

Plate 54, White-fronted Bee-eaters. These birds can be seen quite frequently around Lakes Naivasha and Nakuru in the Rift Valley, hunting for insects, especially bees. They nest in colonies in holes excavated in cliffs or rock-faces. One weekend, when we were staying with friends on a farm at Elmenteita we were fortunate enough to observe such a colony during the breeding season, mating having been triggered off by the long rains. The first day was spent in reconnaissance. We found that the nests were built in the walls of a deep natural fissure in the earth, and it was soon apparent that the light would only be right for photography for about two hours in the early part of the morning. The hide could be set up on a broad ledge on one of the rock-faces; but as we were watching, we saw a Spitting Cobra emerge from one nest hole and make its way into a number of others, this activity continuing for some time. This was a rather unwelcome development as the holes were only about three feet below the ledge, and so invisible to the occupant of the hide. This was the type of excitement I could normally well do without, but since I wanted to make the most of the opportunity, I decided to carry on next day as planned. My wife sat on the opposite lip of the crevice to warn me if the

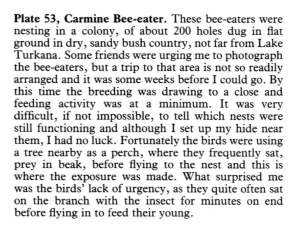

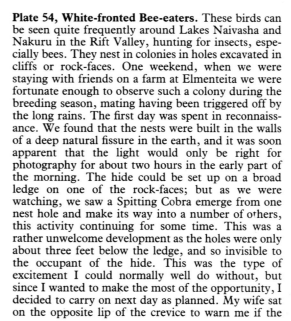

snake emerged. In the event, although it put in an appearance three times, it never came near the hide: but I was quite relieved when the light became unsuitable and I had a good excuse to retire!

Plate 55, Lilac-breasted Roller. I have never found these rollers easy to photograph, in the sense that the beautiful colours registered by the eye hardly ever seemed to reproduce in their true splendour in the transparency. This is mainly due to the fact that the bird was always perched on a branch against a blue or cloudy sky, which spoiled its colours. I think, however, that this particular exposure is quite successful, as the bird had perched lower and therefore grassland formed the background. This picture was obtained by stalking the bird in a car functioning as a mobile hide.

Plate 56, Ground Hornbills. While travelling with Eric and Dorothy Hosking, we had come across a family of these birds one late afternoon. They proved extraordinarily difficult to photograph satisfactorily as they were continuously on the move hunting for food in the tall dry grass. We took a number of recording shots and then moved on to photograph any other subject that might be near a small tributary of the River Mara. Suddenly, to our delight, the family of seven Ground Hornbills came to water at the river and having done so, decided to display, dust bath, preen and generally enjoy themselves. They ignored us completely and we sat there fascinated, and thankful that we had been granted this rare glimpse of their intimate behaviour. It was quite late by now and the exposures were longer than I normally care to use when the subject is moving; but I did manage to get a few worthwhile pictures. Note the distinction in the colour between the bare face and throat of the male on the right and the female behind.

Plate 57, Red-billed Hornbill. Birds which live in the dry bush country around Kilaguni Lodge in Tsavo West National Park have become remarkably tame and it is a matter of continual surprise to me that such normally shy birds as the Golden-breasted Starling and D'Arnaud's Barbet will come to your table on the verandah to share your meal. One can get photographs of a kind, but careful, patient stalking in the grounds of the lodge can be much more rewarding and satisfying. This is how the hornbill was photographed with the 280mm lens.

Plate 58, D'Arnaud's Barbet. A friend and I had set ourselves up near a tree, which seemed a favourite haunt of a number of species, on the wait-and-see-what-happens principle, very much like sitting on a lake shore. Starlings, buffalo-weavers, sparrow-weavers, hornbills and others came, and suddenly this barbet appeared. It moved about rapidly from branch to branch, rarely staying long enough in any one position. A very frustrating experience altogether, but eventually patience paid off. The bird suddenly landed on the ground, went down a hole head first and emerged backwards carrying a dead leaf. It continued this exercise for some time, thus making it possible to make a number of exposures. We later discovered that the hole (at the base of the short upright stem on the right) was its nest, but could not ascertain whether it was in use as there was no feeding activity.

Plate 59, Red-and-Yellow Barbet. One of the main reasons why a friend and I had gone to spend three days at the prehistoric site of Olorgasailie, on the way

to Magadi, was to photograph this barbet. We had been told it was quite tame at the camp there, and thus easy to photograph. To encourage it to make an appearance, I had taken a tape recording of a pair of these birds duetting – characteristic behaviour which is fascinating to hear and also to watch because of the display that accompanies it. We sat with our cameras in what we considered attractive and suitable surroundings and played the tape. The barbets responded without hesitation, but always stayed just too far out of range, and usually behind branches. After two days of fruitless effort we gave up, returned to camp and were just having a consoling beer, when suddenly the barbet appeared right at our feet looking for food scraps. It was not bothered by us in the least and so, although it took a long time to get it in a carefully contrived photogenic situation, we eventually got some reasonable results.

Plates 60 & 61, Red-rumped Swallows, Rosy-breasted Longclaw. Both these are good examples of making the most of an opportunity when it suddenly arises. I was driving very slowly through the Nairobi National Park, keeping a sharp eye open for anything of interest. The swallows were sitting on top of a branch (at the time I did not even know what they were!) and I was attracted by the almost Japanese quality of the picture. Composing it very carefully in the viewfinder, I sited the birds towards the top left hand corner, with the branch leading up to them from the bottom right. The effect was emphasized by the out-of-focus background and the muted tones of the subject and setting. Suddenly, another day, the grassy plains of the open park were alive with flame-coloured birds, flying from one low bush to the next, disappearing in the long grass and then reappearing somewhere else. As soon as a suitable subject was sighted, I drove towards it carefully, making exposures as I got nearer and nearer. Most of the longclaws flew away before I could get close, except this one.

Plate 62, Rueppell's White-crowned Shrike. In the centre of the vast semi-circle of tents at Amboseli Camp is a small thorn tree which seemed to be used as a staging post by a number of birds, during their trips to and from the tall thorn trees on the periphery of the camp. So I set up my hide near it, and waited to see what luck would bring me. This is one of the more rewarding exposures I made.

Plate 63, Northern Pied Babbler. We were delighted to find that these birds had not only appeared in our garden but had started nesting. Over a period of time four different nests were discovered, but in each case they were sited near the top of a dense hedge, in such a position that it would have been impossible to uncover them for photography without making them vulnerable to predation by raptors. However, I set up my hide near two of them in the hope that I would be able to photograph the adults making their way to and from the nest in the process of feeding their young. But I failed to allow for their cunning! They made their way to the nest by the most devious routes, never exposing themselves for a second, and more often than not, when they had fed the chicks, they simply exploded out of the hedge and were gone. Eventually I discovered that they responded vigorously to hearing a recording of their calls being played back to them and this is how the exposure was set up. The speaker was put under the bougainvillea bush, the hide was set about twelve feet away and it only remained to press the shutter when the birds appeared in response to the recording.

185

Plate 64, African Paradise Flycatcher. A friend, who lives in Karen on the outskirts of Nairobi, rang me with the news that a pair of African Paradise Flycatchers were nesting in his garden. The tempting aspect was that the male was the white form, not often seen around Nairobi. Added to that, the nest was about ten feet above ground and the birds were so fearless that a hide would not be necessary. On investigating the site, I found that it would be necessary to erect only a short platform, but that the light under the heavy canopy of leaves was not good. I seriously considered the possibility of using a flash, but decided against it because of the rather artificial effect it produces. I was specially anxious to maintain the enchanting tones of the different coloured leaves in the background, with glimpses of blue sky showing through them. I sat on the platform quite openly with the 280mm lens on a tripod, and the flycatchers ignored me completely. I spent two days making a number of exposures at 1/60th second.

Plate 65, Bronzy Sunbird. Sunbirds are practically impossible to photograph successfully as they flit incessantly from blossom to blossom. I am envious of anyone who manages to make an exposure, with the light just right, to capture the fleeting metallic tones in their feathers. Our previous home had many aloes in the garden and these, when in flower, were most popular with sunbirds. With so many blossoms to choose from, it was impossible to predict where the birds would alight and many a frustrating day was spent trying to capture them on film. Eventually, in desperation, I cut off every aloe flower in the garden with the exception of one, carefully selected because of its suitable background, and set up the hide in front of it. Even then only four shots were sharp!

Plate 66, Streaky Seed-eater. This seed-eater was enticed to the perch by means of a bird-table set up in front of the hide. Once again, an appropriate background had been selected to complement the bird.

Plate 67, Pin-tailed Whydah. Earlier I discussed the possibility of photographing birds in your garden by encouraging them to come to a bird-table. One great advantage of this is that you can choose suitable backgrounds for them. Although you are controlling some of the conditions, the challenge still remains as birds are unpredictable! Species which are attracted by seeds can be made to come to a variety of perches set up in different positions. The branch in this picture was carefully chosen to contrast with the lines of the bird.

Plate 68, Red-naped Widow-bird. This branch was selected and carefully placed, to show off the magnificent tail feathers of this widow-bird. The female of this species is much smaller and less colourful.

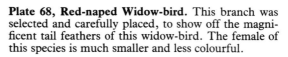

Plate 69, Holub's Golden Weaver. This weaver, always most attractive, but especially so in its full breeding plumage, was photographed late one afternoon in my garden as it waited its turn for seed on the nearby bird-table. The evening light has enhanced still further the glorious quality of its golden plumage.

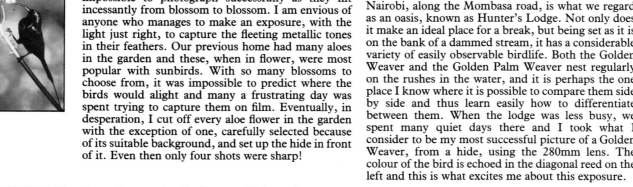
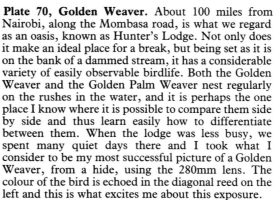

Plate 70, Golden Weaver. About 100 miles from Nairobi, along the Mombasa road, is what we regard as an oasis, known as Hunter's Lodge. Not only does it make an ideal place for a break, but being set as it is on the bank of a dammed stream, it has a considerable variety of easily observable birdlife. Both the Golden Weaver and the Golden Palm Weaver nest regularly on the rushes in the water, and it is perhaps the one place I know where it is possible to compare them side by side and thus learn easily how to differentiate between them. When the lodge was less busy, we spent many quiet days there and I took what I consider to be my most successful picture of a Golden Weaver, from a hide, using the 280mm lens. The colour of the bird is echoed in the diagonal reed on the left and this is what excites me about this exposure.

Plate 71, White-headed Buffalo Weaver. Another early-morning photograph, the result of patient stalking with the hand-held 280mm lens. The best method for taking this sort of shot is to approach slowly without making any sudden or jerky movement, taking two or three steps and stopping, before making the next cautious advance.

Plate 72, Superb Starling. This species is quite tame and common in many areas, and because it is so colourful it certainly qualifies as one of the most photographed birds in Africa! Not that I have either seen or taken many outstanding pictures of it: it is usually spotted on the ground, and shooting down on the subject is not an ideal camera angle. This is one of my more successful efforts and was taken from a hide; the bird was at eye-level, standing on a tree stump where I was photographing the site of a woodpecker's nest. The light was just right, showing a myriad of iridescent colours in its plumage; the transparency was overexposed by about half a stop to record them. 'Superb' is certainly an apt name for this bird.

Bibliography

Brown, L. (1973). *The Mystery of the Flamingos*, new and expanded ed. Nairobi, E. A. Publishing House.

Brown, L. H. (1958). The breeding of the Greater Flamingo *Phoenicopterus ruber* at Lake Elmenteita, Kenya Colony. *Ibis* 100: 388–420.

Brown, L. and Amadon, D. (1968). *Eagles, hawks and falcons of the world*. London, Country Life Books.

Brown, L. H., Powell-Cotton, D. and Hopcraft, J. B. D. (1973). The breeding of the Greater Flamingo and the Great White Pelican in East Africa. *Ibis* 115: 367–374.

Brown, L. H. and Root, A. (1971). The breeding behavior of the Lesser Flamingo *Pheoniconaias minor*. *Ibis* 113: 147–172.

Brown, L. H. and Urban, E. K. (1969). The breeding biology of the Great White Pelican *Pelecanus onocrotalus roseus* at Lake Shala, Ethiopia. *Ibis* 111: 199–237.

Chapin, J. P. (1932). The birds of the Belgian Congo. *Bulletin of the American Museum of Natural History* vol. 65.

Eastman, R. (1969). *The Kingfisher*. London, Collins.

Forbes-Watson, A. D. (1971). *Skeleton Checklist of East African Birds*. Nairobi (duplicated).

Godders, J. ed. *Birds of the World*, 9 vols. London, I.P.C.

Grossman, M. L. and Hamlet, J. (1965). *Birds of prey of the world*. London, Cassell.

Grzimek, B. editor-in-chief. (1968). *Grzimek's animal life encyclopaedia*, Eng. Ed. vols. 7, 8 and 9. London, Van Nostrand Reinhold.

Hopcraft, J. B. D. *Baharini Wildlife Sanctuary annual report, 1973–1974*. Nairobi (duplicated).

Jackson, F. J. (1938). *The birds of Kenya Colony and the Uganda Protectorate*. 3 vols. London, Gurney and Jackson.

Kahl, M. P. (1968). Recent breeding records of storks in Eastern Africa. *Journal of the East Africa Natural History Society and National Museum* 116: 67–72.

Mackworth-Praed, C. W. and Grant, C. H. B. (1952 & 1955). *African handbook of birds*. Series I, vols. 1 & 2. *Birds of eastern and north eastern Africa*. London, Longmans Green & Co.

Moreau, R. E. (1966). *The bird faunas of Africa and its islands*. London, Academic Press.

Moreau, R. E. (1972). *The Palaearctic-African bird migratory systems*. London, Academic Press.

Moreau, R. E. and W. M. (1941). Breeding biology of the Silvery-cheeked Hornbill. *Auk* 58: 13–27.

Morgan, W. T. N. Ed. (1972). *East Africa: its people and resources*. Nairobi, Oxford University Press.

North, M. E. W. (1963). Breeding of the Black-headed Herons at Nairobi, Kenya 1958–62. *Journal of the East Africa Natural History Society and Coryndon Museum* 106: 34–63.

Ojany, F. F. (1971). The geography of East Africa. *Zamani: a survey of East African history*. eds. Ogot, B. A. and Kieran, J. A., pp. 22–48, 3rd imp. Nairobi, E. A. Publishing House.

Reynolds, J. F. (1974). Nursery helps for bee-eaters. *Wildlife* 16: 256–259.

Reynolds, J. F. (1974). Barbets of the African savannahs. *Wildlife* 16: 464–469.

Reynolds, J. F. (1975). Coursers of the dry savannahs. *Wildlife* 16: 274–278.

Root, J. and A. (1969). Inside a hornbill's walled-up nest. *National Geographic Magazine*. 136: 846–855.

Thomson, A. L. ed. (1964). *A new dictionary of birds*. London, Nelson.

Van Someren, V. D. (1958). *A bird watcher in Kenya*. London, Oliver & Boyd.

Van Someren, V. G. L. (1956). Days with birds. *Fieldiana: zoology*. Chicago Natural History Museum, vol. 38.

Williams, J. G. (1963). *A field guide to the birds of East and Central Africa*. London, Collins.

Williams, J. G. (1967). *A field guide to the National Parks of East Africa*. London, Collins.

Index